CW01191666

YEARS OF ENDURANCE

To
My Wife

YEARS OF ENDURANCE

LIFE ABOARD THE BATTLECRUISER *TIGER* 1914–16

SURGEON REAR ADMIRAL
JOHN R MUIR

New Introduction By
MIKE FARQUHARSON-ROBERTS

Seaforth
PUBLISHING

Introduction copyright © Mike Farquharson-Roberts 2021
Type format of this edition © Seaforth Publishing

This edition published in Great Britain in 2021 by
Seaforth Publishing,
A division of Pen & Sword Books Ltd,
47 Church Street,
Barnsley S70 2AS

www.seaforthpublishing.com

First published by Philip Allan 1937

British Library Cataloguing in Publication Data
A catalogue record for this book is available from the British Library

ISBN 978 1 3990 1720 6 (HARDBACK)
ISBN 978 1 3990 1722 0 (KINDLE)
ISBN 978 1 3990 1721 3 (EPUB)

All rights reserved. No part of this publication may be reproduced or transmitted in any form or by any means, electronic or mechanical, including photocopying, recording, or any information storage and retrieval system, without prior permission in writing of the above publisher.

Pen & Sword Books Limited incorporates the imprints of Atlas, Archaeology, Aviation, Discovery, Family History, Fiction, History, Maritime, Military, Military Classics, Politics, Select, Transport, True Crime, Air World, Frontline Publishing, Leo Cooper, Remember When, Seaforth Publishing, The Praetorian Press, Wharncliffe Local History, Wharncliffe Transport, Wharncliffe True Crime and White Owl.

Typeset and designed by Mac Style
Printed and bound in Great Britain by CPI Group (UK) Ltd, Croydon, CR0 4YY

Contents

List of Illustrations		vi
New Introduction		vii
Prologue		xii
Chapter I	Mobilisation	1
Chapter II	A Temporary Hospital	12
Chapter III	Our Ship	31
Chapter IV	Our Officers	49
Chapter V	Scarborough	86
Chapter VI	The Dogger	100
Chapter VII	At Rosyth	116
Chapter VIII	The North Sea	131
Chapter IX	Jutland	147
Chapter X	The M.O. in Action	162
Chapter XI	Aftermath	177
Chapter XII	Jack at War	187
Epilogue		200

List of Illustrations

1. *Tiger* at Roysth, 1914.
2. HMS *Tiger*, showing alterations made after the war.
3. A direct hit on a turret (HMS *Tiger*).
4. *Tiger* in action (Jutland, 31st May, 1916).
5. The last of the *Queen Mary*, 31st May, 1916.
6. The writer.
7. The wreck of the *Invincible*, 31st May, 1916.
8. A direct hit on an armour plate (HMS *Tiger*).

New Introduction

Naval medical officers have received little attention from either historians or novelists and biographers. Once the story of scurvy and the introduction of lemon juice are out of the way, the major works of naval history barely mention medicine or the navy's surgeons. The best known naval medical officer must be the fictional Stephen Maturin of Patrick O'Brian's series of novels set during the Napoleonic Wars, and he was given added allure by doubling as a spy. So this new edition of John Muir's book, describing his experiences as a relatively junior medical officer during the early years of the First World War, rights a significant omission in the naval literature of the era. But the book offers much more than medical insight for it paints perhaps one of the most vivid pictures of life in Royal Navy battlecruiser to have come out of the war.

Though he never explicitly explains his rank in the book, John Muir was likely a 'Staff Surgeon' during the period he is writing about (he ultimately became a Surgeon Rear Admiral). A doctor in the Royal Navy had (and still has) a singular position in some ways, sitting somewhere halfway between the chaplain and the other officers, and this position is recognised as such, giving him unique status, being far closer to the lower deck (the term used to describe the non-officer part of the crew) than the rest of the officers. He was also bound by medical confidentiality and inevitably knew things about his patients (the entire company) that others did not. This meant that, in addition to their primary duties, he and the chaplain were effectively the ship's welfare officers.

Muir was not only a qualified doctor but also a sailor. As well as *Years of Endurance*, he wrote a many-times reprinted book *Messing about in Boats*, a memoir of his yachting days as a young man. So this book is by someone who knows the sea, and was finally to die at sea. When the Second World War broke out, he had retired from the navy and, being 67, was not recalled to service as a medical officer. However, he was commissioned into the Royal Naval Volunteer Reserve as a Sub-Lieutenant and was appointed to HMS *Campeador*, a private steam yacht taken into the navy for patrol service. She was commanded by retired Commander Davey (Master of the Dartmoor foxhounds) with the erstwhile owner Mr McAndrew and John Muir as two of the officers. After some months they were both promoted to Lieutenant, but were killed when *Campeador* was destroyed by a magnetic mine off Portsmouth in June 1940.

The opening part of the book is fascinating. The author was working in the Chatham sickbay, the medical facility, and describes well the tumultuous days around the outbreak of war and the mobilisation of the reserves, as well as the setting up of an emergency hospital for the anticipated casualties which, it was thought, would overwhelm the existing naval hospital. Having had to do the same, albeit afloat in RFA *Fort Grange*, in the lead up to the first Gulf War, I recognise the problems he faced, though I was spared the induction of large numbers of reservists. Furthermore, I was fortunate in having the experience of predecessors to work on and a full scale of stores devised for the job. Muir did not. The Royal Navy had not been at war for a very long time, so he was 'flying blind'.

He then went from Chatham to be the senior medical officer in the brand new battlecruiser HMS *Tiger*. She was the culmination of Admiral Fisher's vision, fast, heavily armed but not as heavily armoured as a Dreadnought battleship.

NEW INTRODUCTION

She was the first battlecruiser to be fitted with director fire control for her main armament, which allowed the big guns to be controlled from a central point high up in the ship. She was technically the most capable and advanced battlecruiser in the world. But with the outbreak of war, she was rushed into service. It has been suggested by some that her bad performance at the Battle of Dogger Bank was due to her being largely manned by 'the sweepings of the naval barracks' including many 'recovered deserters', namely poorly disciplined and motivated sailors. Muir paints a very different picture, however, of well-motivated but inexperienced men.

He also paints a vivid picture of a ship straight out of the builder's yard. Normally, the builders would be required to clean a ship before the navy took her over, and this was far more than just polishing the bright work. During building it was the usual practice for workman to use a ship as a latrine, but because of the haste, it was left to *Tiger*'s ship's company to clean up the quite extensive fouling, all the while trying to get the ship ready to go to war, something Muir considered a genuine health risk. Quite recently, I visited the new HMS *Queen Elizabeth* in build and noted a line of Portaloos in the hangar for the builder's workmen – a modern solution to an obvious problem. To make matters worse *Tiger* was not afforded the normal period to shakedown as a ship's company, while the time to work up to fighting efficiency was very also curtailed. As a result, and according to the historian Arthur Marder, she only fired her guns for the first time at a moving target at the Battle of the Dogger Bank; and not surprisingly, she did not shoot well. Muir was obviously extremely proud of his ship and her people, and felt they were hard done by. It is obvious that he knew his ship, and more importantly, its people, the sailors of the lower deck, and there are many anecdotes, some amusing, some thought provoking; at one point he is consulted by a sailor whose wife is being evicted because their landlord can extract more rent from a munitions worker

Muir then describes the Battle of Jutland, firstly as a semi-fictionalised account of an early part of the action to put the events into context and then from the medical point of view. What would now be called the medical organisation for action is entirely recognisable today, above all the pressure on the medical staff, working continuously for many hours treating casualties in an open space behind the ship's armour. At the end he returned to his sick bay (outside the armour protection) and found nothing. It had been destroyed by a shell hit.

Medicine in the Royal Navy was well advanced by contemporary standards and it is surprising how much of what he describes is still relevant today. There is in the Admiralty Library a medical officer's journal from another ship covering the Battle of Jutland which includes an X-ray of a fractured femur (thigh bone) taken during the action. X-rays had been introduced to medical practice just before the turn of the century and in 1916 were not widely used elsewhere. In a recent book *Fittest of the Fit* (Seaforth 2019) Kevin Brown looks at medicine in the Navy in the Second World War, which built on the experience from the First World War and shows how the Navy remained a leading body in British medicine.

Muir is careful, even fastidious, about naming names. He does not name his messmates, and apart from Admirals Beatty and Jellicoe, even his superiors. He obviously felt Admiral Battenburg, sacked by Churchill as First Sea Lord, was badly treated, but he does not name Churchill and nor, despite his obvious distaste, his successor, Admiral Fisher. His opinions offer a fascinating insight into the opinions and feelings of the Navy, which was very much 'the silent service'. There are so many books and memoirs about the war on land at this time, but this is an invaluable and almost unique insight into the life of the Royal Navy afloat in the Great War.

Mike Farquharson-Roberts CBE PhD (Mar Hist) FRCS

There is beauty in the bellow of the blast,
There is grandeur in the growling of the gale,
There is eloquent outpouring,
When the lion is a-roaring,
And the tiger is a-lashing of his tail.
The Mikado, by W S Gilbert.

Quoted by Admiral Beatty in a speech to the ship's company of the *Tiger* after the Dogger action.

Prologue

Ye gentlemen of England!
That sit at home at ease,
Oh! little do you think upon
The dangers of the seas.

Out in the wild North Sea, two hundred miles from the nearest land, and that the land of the foe, His Majesty's battle cruisers, head to wind, are steaming at the reduced speed of 10 knots. We do not expect to meet the German Fleet in force, but there are 'enterprises directed towards the North' of his that it is our duty to bring to naught, and for the last two days, as for the next two, we have been accomplishing it by the mere terror of our presence. This is a test of endurance, the seamen of England against the soldiers on board ships of Germany.

Down below in my cabin I sit with my chair securely jammed, and hang on to the writing-table with one hand. In this box of white painted steel, measuring only 10 feet by 8 feet by 7 feet, I live and move and have my separate being from the rest of the mess. This cabin is one of the few provided with natural daylight – imagine, if you can, what the absence of that privilege means! – and is plainly furnished with a bunk having drawers underneath, a writing-table, a chair, and a folding washstand. In spite of my solitary scuttle, the use of the two electric lights on such a day as this is absolutely necessary. For two years and more this has been my home – wet sometimes, cold often, comfortless always.

The stern of the ship rises with a mighty heave, and the whole vessel vibrates furiously to the wriggle of our four propellers. Then down and down she sinks until there is an ominous pause in the movement, and the scuttle is buried in the grey-green sea, so that only the electric lights save me from utter darkness. Overhead I can hear the crash of hundreds of tons of water falling upon our quarter-deck. Then as the heave is repeated, combined with a sideways jerk and a roll that sends me trundling on to the deck, I can hear through the enormous thickness of the ship's steel sides the Niagara of water as it hastens back to the ocean whence it came. The sound of falling water and the swish, swaash, swish, as it sweeps across the deck outside my cabin remind me that it is time to get my sea-boots on. So far the water is only two inches deep, but when it rises to the height of my eight-inch door coaming my cabin will be flooded. The water goes on steadily rising, and I clear my lower drawers in preparation for what I know is coming.

The ship stops, shudders, gasps, and then with a rapidly rolling motion glides down into the trough of the sea. Instinctively I grip at the table with one hand, whilst with the other I attempt to stay the flood of opening drawers which are emptying their contents on to the floor. Stupidly enough I have forgotten to lock them. Somehow or other I get them filled up and replaced, remembering this time to turn the key.

The hatches and ventilators on deck have all been battened down to prevent them from being filled with salt water as they are submerged beneath the waves, so of course the fans have been stopped and there has been no fresh-air supply to my cabin for over twenty-four hours. The atmosphere below is damp and almost unbreathable. One is heavy and stupid from carbonic acid gas poisoning. I have to sleep – yes! that is the word, *sleep!* – here to-night, so the less I continue to foul the limited supply of air the better. But where to go?

Anyhow, I must get some fresh air.

Sea-legs? I've had sea-legs for twenty years, but now I might just as well have wooden ones. The seas outside are averaging about 20 feet in height, and three every two minutes. The ship is rolling through an angle of 18 to 27 degrees, the latter being about the slope of the ordinary roof. These seas are short and jerky in the North Sea, where the shallow waters and confined space prevent the long smooth swell such as is found in the Atlantic, and over which we should ride in absolute comfort. Just imagine the room of the ordinary house rising bodily in the air for a distance of 20 feet every forty seconds, whilst in the same time the sides of the floor are alternately depressed and elevated through an arc of 20 degrees – a distance on this ship of 16 feet. During twenty seconds the slope is towards you, and for the other twenty you are looking down a steep hill. At the maximum of each motion walking is impossible. The only method of progression is by taking a few short steps at the end of each pitch-roll-heave, and on my skill in forecasting the incidence and duration of this period depends my immunity from serious injury. At the end of these short dashes I jam myself against a bulkhead, feeling lucky if I can get hold of the edges of a cabin doorway, which all the demons of the storm seem to be wrenching from my straining fingers. If I fail to seize hold of anything or am forced to let go, I sit down in the water in the passage at once to prevent myself being jerked like a stone from a catapult against the opposite bulkhead. Occasionally I make an error, and for days afterwards I shall feel the effects of the specially hardened steel which butts and bruises my breathless body.

After having advanced about 50 feet in five minutes, I wonder whether it is worth while going on. But the recollection of my cabin atmosphere warns me that if to go on is to get hurt, to go back is to be sick. Yes, sick! The sea, in all its power and majesty, from a typhoon in the Formosa Channel to a full gale amidst the mountainous rollers off Cape Leeuwin, has done its worst to make me sick, and failed. What the sea alone could not do, my dog-kennel could manage in five minutes with as little difficulty as if I had swallowed an emetic. And – I've got to sleep there to-night or take my chance on the upper mess-decks in a foot of water. Ugh!

I meet another officer in the narrow passage, and warily we watch one another like a couple of professional wrestlers manoeuvring for an opening. Somehow or other we pass, he with a scratch on one side of his mouth and I with a wild stamp on my foot. As we balance for the fraction of a minute afterwards he shouts cheerily, 'Who would sell a farm and go to sea?' 'Harley Street and a good bedside manner for me!' I reply, and we stagger apart.

Our ships are built to fight, and after that – oh! a long way after that – to live in. Over two years of warfare have perfectly satisfied me as to their grim efficiency for the work we have at present in hand. But if I could get hold of the constructor who designed that ladder and hatchway, I could wish him no worse than to see him going up before me. Luckily the ladder has fairly open rungs, and, provided they are strongly enough fastened to withstand my efforts at tearing them away from the steel bulkhead, I ought to manage all right.

At last I am more or less in the open, breathing deep, welcome draughts of the purest air that man can know, laden with salt spray though it is. I am more or less sheltered from the full fury of the wind by the steel superstructure surrounding the lower part of the forebridge and looking down over the after part of the ship.

There is a leaden, lowering sky overhead, fringed as it meets the horizon by a band of steel-grey luminous mist.

No movement is visible on that pall that shrouds the sun. Its immensity presses on the world and the brain contemplating it, threatening to crush both in its suggestion of ineffable gloom. Streaks of dark smoke are driven downwards into the sea from our funnels. Impelled by the angry blows of the storm gigantic waves rush madly past us, rearing with pain until, seeking to hide from the merciless hand that hunts them, they disappear under a smother of foam. They meet the ship in their course and, furious at this new obstacle which impedes their escape, break over and attempt to overwhelm her. Labouring heavily and jerkily, the ship raises first one side and then the other to her implacable enemy, which, balked in its efforts at crushing, dives under and by main force tries to heave her over. The open deck is a death-trap on which the swirling waters seem to be eagerly seeking the fool who would dare to attempt a crossing.

I am looking on at the most titanic struggle that ever takes place – a struggle which is so much a part of my life that its import barely attracts my attention. The most powerful and costly instrument made by man and, with one exception, the most destructive agency of the forces of nature, are joined in combat.

And down below on the sodden mess-deck a group of stokers are discussing the question of – leave! What else is there to discuss? Food? The galley has long ago been swamped out, and dry bread and a slice of corned beef are all they are likely to see for the next twenty-four hours. Sleep? The mess-decks have a foot of water on them, and the slung hammocks are banging with great, vicious whacks either against the bulkheads or the man lying alongside. Their clothing is wet and filthy; they are sick or hungry, or both; they are overworked, tired, and sleepy; they are living in unimaginable misery; they are smarting under the recollection of the loafer on shore who has stepped into their jobs and is walking out with their best girls. So they

PROLOGUE

are discussing the question dearest to the sailorman's heart. And as a specially heavy sea breaks in through the chinks in the gun port and souses them thoroughly for the twentieth time that day, these inexpressible lunatics burst into a roar of laughter and shout 'Do it again!'

Chapter I
Mobilisation

The preliminary mobilisation of May 1914 was over and done with and as Senior Medical Officer of the Barracks at Chatham I was not surprised when told that the Commander-in-Chief at the Nore wanted to see me. The C-in-C was Sir Richard Poore, a former commanding officer of mine. He was a singularly able man with an uncanny knack of laying his finger on the weak spots of any organisation, but very easy to approach and at all times helpful and understanding in his appreciation of difficulties. In my own mind I had no doubt that he was going to 'put me on the mat'.

'I have sent for you to discuss your mobilisation arrangements. What do you think of them?'

I have always felt much more inclined to go on the mat myself than be put there by anyone, so I answered 'They were rotten, Sir!'

He cast a keen appraising look at me. Then he spoke a little stiffly.

'Exactly what I meant to tell you, though not perhaps in these same words. Your department held up the mobilisation all the time. Your medical examinations of the drafts were not carried out as they ought to have been, and there was unnecessary and dangerous delay in getting the men kitted up and sent to their ships. Your explanation, please?'

'Shortage of staff, Sir.'

'But, on paper at any rate, you have plenty of staff.'

'I know that, Sir; but the difficulty is that on the order "Mobilise" the reserves come tumbling into the depot at once and my mobilised people may or may not arrive along with them. If there is any delay in their arrival my small peace-time staff has to carry on as best they can. In this last mobilisation 75% of my people found it impossible to turn up until the mobilisation had been going on for a couple of days, and they had to attack arrears of work instead of finding things working smoothly. In a real mobilisation we shall probably be in a still worse case, as the numbers are bound to be much larger. When the officers who have war appointments to the depot have reported themselves, the staff will be adequate; but there is an awkward period when the men are arriving in large numbers' and as yet the medical officers are adrift.'

'Why haven't you reported this before? You ought to have foreseen it.'

'The mobilisation was carried out according to the Admiralty Instructions turned over to me. I guessed there might be some difficulty, but until the test mobilisation was carried out I had no means of ascertaining how serious the shortage would prove to be.'

'Have you any idea how to get over the difficulty in case of mobilisation for war?'

'Yes, Sir. I have a scheme in my mind which should prove satisfactory. I propose to arrange with the medical men in Rochester and Chatham that they should be available for temporary duty in the Barracks until the arrival of our own people renders their further employment unnecessary. There are numberless other minor alterations in the routine necessary; but supply of medical men is the most important.'

'That sounds feasible. You had better submit to me through the Commodore a report on the test mobilisation and your plan for improving it. I shall forward it to the Admiralty for approval since it will mean spending money, and they will want to keep anything involving expenditure under their control.'

I went back to the Commodore under whom I was serving and told him the result of the interview. Of course, the whole subject had been discussed between us over and over again, both during the mobilisation, when my department was obviously breaking down, and since. He was a short, bearded man, with a humorous twinkle and a limp – a legacy from the Boer War when he had been shot in the hip. He had accused me on more than one occasion of not only being anxious to make my point but also to ram it into his ribs, a procedure which he assured me was quite unnecessary. He told me that the success of my scheme depended entirely on the willing co-operation of the local medical men and until that was assured it was little use arranging for anything else.

Guessing that I was most likely to find the civilian doctors free about 9 p.m. I rang up half a dozen whose names I found in the telephone book and asked them: 'In case of mobilisation for war would you be prepared to report at very short notice in the Barracks and remain there for about a week, your whole time being employed in the physical examination of drafts of men? You would be accommodated and fed in the officers' mess.'

Five out of the six assented eagerly, only asking for an hour or two of grace so that they could arrange for the conduct of their private practices. The sixth, who had acknowledged my ring in the accents of Cork was so long in making a reply that I thought he had been cut off. But when I shouted through the telephone 'Are you there?' I got the unexpected answer 'And phwat will be the remuneration' The question had already been discussed with the Commodore, so I said 'Three guineas a day' 'I'll come!' and the interview was over. My scheme was drawn up and handed to the Commander-in-Chief. That officer sent it to the Admiralty, who just ignored it.

It had struck someone in authority at the Admiralty that if we had an action in the North Sea and there were a large number of wounded it might seriously strain the accommodation of the Royal Naval Hospital, which was usually pretty well filled with the normal sick list of the Fleet. As a large number of the hospital patients are semi-convalescents it was supposed to be a brain wave that they should be discharged to the barracks and attended by the medical officers of that establishment. So to add to my worries and the Commodore's difficulties the latter was ordered to detail a block for equipment as a hospital and I was to forward a complete inventory of the equipment that would be required to deal with about 200 patients. The Commodore was annoyed, because he knew that on mobilisation it would be almost impossible to spare a block which could accommodate over 500 fighting men, and I was appalled at the casual manner in which I was supposed to be able to rhyme off the equipment for a hospital of 200 beds starting off from nothing. If I were lavish I should get cursed by the Treasury: if I were niggardly I should be considered incompetent by my own people. In either case I was riding for a particularly nasty fall. The only comfort was that I knew the Commodore and the Commander-in-Chief would back me up through thick and thin, so I went ahead and buried myself in the details of knives and forks, sheets and surgical dressings.

When finished I took my reams of foolscap to the Commodore, and he turned over my pages listlessly.

'Where do my men come in whom I shall want to sleep here?' he said.

Looking back on these days it is plain now that we were all living in a state of highly strung expectation of something – we could hardly have said what. We had guessed for years, and been certain since Agadir, that the Germans meant to make an effort at world domination and that to effect that ambition it was necessary to wipe out Britain as a world power. We knew also the simple truth of Lord Roberts's statement that Germany would strike when Germany's hour had struck. Jingoism is not and never has been a characteristic of the British Navy, but we felt fairly sure that Germany's only chance of success against our Fleet was by one of those lightning attacks when we were most assured of peace, and that such an attack would be the first declaration of war. That she would attack France again on any old excuse just as she had done in 1870 was a foregone conclusion, and that when she had hammered France into bits she would take us in her stride was the belief of many of the thinking ones amongst us.

At the end of July came the order to prepare to mobilise, and I was in a quandary. Was I to attempt the old discredited scheme of mobilisation, or could I get permission to carry out my own scheme which at least promised some degree of efficiency? It looked as if the mobilisation, and this time a real one, was going to be held up because I dare not, without authority, incur the expenditure of £100. The Commodore rang up the Commander-in-Chief, who in his turn assaulted the Admiralty. Men were already arriving in large batches; soon they would pour over us in a flood. I was getting more and more anxious and almost inclined to accept the risk of adopting my own scheme without authority; but the Commodore would not hear of it. Then a telegram was handed to me stating my scheme had been approved and was to be adopted. A telephone message to my medical friends brought them into the barracks at the double, and the hectic activity of suddenly raising the numbers in the barracks from its normal quota of 6,000 to over 30,000 was in full swing.

The men arrived by every possible conveyance, from their own legs upwards. The trams which ran from Chatham Railway station to just outside the barracks were commandeered, and anyone who wished could have a free ride. London buses for transport purposes were arriving every hour of the day and night, and were parked in the barracks recreation grounds.

There was a little incident on the night of 4th August. We had had no time to look at the papers and we hardly knew what was happening in the outside world at all. It was true that on the evening of the 1st August the Commodore had told his heads about 6 o'clock that we were at war, but that had been cancelled by another statement a couple of hours later. This first statement had been given under a seal of secrecy for some reason which we could not fathom. We hoped it meant the Navy was going to get its blow in first. On the night of the 4th a message was passed round the heads of departments that the Commodore wished to see them in his office as convenient. I finished some work I was doing, knocked at his door and entered. He was sitting in his chair in front of his desk doing nothing for the first time since I had known him, and his gaze was fixed on a large clock on the wall which showed the time to be 12.20. Apparently he had not noticed my knock or my entrance and I stood at his elbow for a moment before I called his attention to my presence with the usual 'You sent for me, Sir'. With not a trace of his usual friendly greeting which made it a joy to work under him he slowly withdrew his gaze from the clock, and speaking mechanically as if the words were being forced from him said, 'I have to inform you that war was declared with Germany at midnight.' His words beat upon my brain but conveyed nothing to me, nothing at all. His gaze went back to the clock as if he wanted by an effort of will to call back those fleeting twenty minutes. I said 'Yes, Sir,' and waited, doubtful whether the interview was over or not. With an effort he brought himself back to his endless duties and asked me how my arrangements were progressing. 'Everything is perfectly satisfactory, Sir.' Another officer knocked at the door and I passed out as he entered.

The medical men were each given a corner of the drill shed, where, behind a screen, they examined the newcomers and gave an opinion as to whether they were fit to be drafted to a ship, fit for shore service only, or useless. I warned them all, civilians as well as Service men: 'This is not an examination of newly joined recruits. These men are all trained men and we shall need every one who can possibly serve in any capacity. Shut your eyes to everything except impossible disabilities, and do not entirely reject anybody without referring the case to me.'

The civilian doctors were wonderful. Day after day and night after night, in a foetid atmosphere on these hot August nights, they stuck to their duties until I was compelled to interfere and send them to the mess for some sleep and food. My friend from Cork who, I found out afterwards, had been practising amongst the lowest slums of Chatham, started by examining each man as if he were a clinical case in a Hospital and took about an hour over each one. After I had explained things to him and what was wanted he went to the other extreme and paid more attention to the warlike enthusiasm of the examinee than his bronchial and heart sounds. And when at 4 o'clock one morning I found him working away worn and dogged and ordered him to be relieved and go back to the mess, all the thanks I got was 'Faith, this is a gentleman's life. Go to bed yourself!'

Wandering round the drafts one night and generally keeping an eye on things my attention was attracted by an unusual spectacle. It was that of a tall man perfectly dressed in the Bond Street garb of the day, silk hat, morning coat, beautifully creased trousers, spats and pointed shoes. I wondered what he was doing amongst the rather uncouth mob who filled the drill shed and finally put him down as someone from the civilian departments of the Admiralty. He looked at me once or twice as I passed near him as if he wished to speak to me, and at last when I was free he came up and addressed me in a language whose accents agreed with his costume.

'I've been told you are the P.M.O. of the barracks, Sir.'

'Yes, I am.'

'I wish you would help me to join up.'

This was a facer. He must be one of the volunteers, but if so he had no business in the drill shed.

'You'd better go to the recruiting office. All these men here are old Service hands rejoining.'

'But I am an old Service hand, Sir.'

'What's your difficulty, then?'

'I left after my twelve years service about eight years ago and did not join the Fleet Reserve, and the drafting people say they can't trace me.'

'What was your rating?'

The old formula came quick and fast from his lips. 'Petty Officer first class; two badges; turret gunlayer first class.' A prize in any ship.

'What can I do?'

'I thought if you spoke to the drafting people they might accept my word for it and put me through. They can verify all this at any time.'

I went straight up to the nearest bench where the drafting corporal was busy ticking off the new arrivals.

'Can you put this Petty Officer through? His papers are adrift.'

'Certainly, Sir,' said the corporal' 'Particulars, please,' to the petty officer.

The last I saw of him was when an hour or so later he was being stripped to pass the Medical Officer.

I had completely forgotten the incident when about a fortnight later the Commodore sent for me and asked me whether I could help in tracing a man about whom enquiries were being made by the Admiralty. It seemed that an important oil fuel firm which had large pumping stations on the Thames was in great trouble because the man who had charge of all their berths and docking arrangements had disappeared and, in wartime at any rate, he was irreplaceable. Nobody knew what had happened to him as he had simply walked out of his office one day, but the firm knew that he had been a petty officer in the navy and they suspected he had rejoined. The Admiralty added a note that if found the man was to be released at once and returned to his job, which, incidentally, carried a salary of £800 a year. As I read the letter there flitted through my mind a recollection of the top-hatted gentleman, and once a lead was given it was easy enough to trace the entry, and my surmise proved to be correct. Shortly afterwards a very disgruntled petty officer who had been happily serving on a light cruiser in the North Sea was dragged back to his job of berthing oilers.

The arrangements made before the War for accommodating semi-convalescents had been completed and 180 patients from the Naval Hospital were discharged to my improvised wards in the barracks. It was a stupid arrangement as it encroached fearfully on the limited space available for ordinary barrack purposes, but strong representations made to the Admiralty were of no avail. There they were and there they had to remain. One day the Commodore sent for me and dropped a bombshell. His old humorous twinkle had come back and he eyed me amusedly.

'Evidently your people don't think I have enough trouble competing with a two-and-a-half striper. They are sending down a four-striper to frighten me.'

It was the first news I had had that I was to be superseded. He named my successor and asked me whether I knew him. I did not, although I knew his reputation. He was considered to be a great administrator by the Admiralty on account of his flair for niggling detail. Of course I said nothing of this to the Commodore, but merely asked whether I was to be relieved. His answer was that he had refused to consider my removal until the new arrival had a thorough grip of the job. The outlook did not seem promising.

The new man came and proceeded with much energy to make himself conversant with the Depot duties. As there were nearly twenty junior medical officers under me, a large Sick Bay, a temporary hospital with 180 patients, heavy drafting going on every day and reams of paper work from the Admiralty, it took a long time for him to grasp what was being done, especially as he insisted on knowing the tiniest details connected with every department. Finally he dropped into my chair in the P.M.O.'s office, stated that he was prepared to take control of everything, and that until I was relieved I was to act as his senior assistant. It was the ordinary Service routine and suited me admirably as I had not had my clothes off except to take a bath since the mobilisation had started.

Able man though he was the War had found out the weak spot in his mental equipment. The job had become much too big for one man to pretend he could control every little ramification of it although he tried to do so, with disastrous results. I pleaded with him to allow the junior officers the full responsibilities of their respective duties and, if they failed him, to clear them out and employ others in their places. He refused; and finally gave me a written order that not a single decision was to be taken on any subject even remotely concerned with the medical department without it being referred to him for approval. As the result of that order I had him out of bed eleven times the first night it was in force. In the morning he cancelled the order and said officers were to use their discretion. They used their discretion, and were invariably told they were wrong. The situation was impossible. I went to the Commodore and was told I must carry out the orders of my superior officer. It was the only answer possible in the service and I ought to have known it.

Meanwhile the congestion in the barracks was getting worse and worse, and I began to fear the outbreak of an epidemic of some kind – cerebrospinal meningitis being the bugbear of all medical officers in these conditions. Men were sleeping on buses, those on the top deck sheltering under the waterproof sheets which covered the seats, sleeping in corridors and doorways, sleeping in over-crowded tents erected on the recreation ground, sleeping in the drill shed, sleeping in doorways and garden paths. One night the Commander asked me to inspect with him one of the rooms in the blocks which was supposed to be capable of housing a maximum of 168 men. We counted 600 lying in every possible and impossible position in an atmosphere which felt solid as you walked through the room. And one complete block was being used for hospital purposes!

Chapter II
A Temporary Hospital

The Commodore sent for me.

'I have received permission from the Admiralty to open a temporary hospital. Go down to the Welcome Sailors' Hostel and come back and tell me whether you think it can be converted into an hospital, and how long it will take to do it. I am sending you in charge.'

I went to the Hostel and saw the Wesleyan minister who was in charge of it. He listened to what I had to say and then showed me over the building. I made many enquiries and when they were answered satisfactorily made up my mind. The place would do and I told the minister. He was not too well pleased, as he said it meant the end of much useful work. I suggested it might be the beginning of it and he agreed. He wanted a week to turn over in so I gave him twenty-four hours. What would he do about his staff? I told him I would take them over as cooks and attendants until such time as other arrangements were made. He then suggested we should pay him £60 a week for the use of the building. The reply was that I had nothing to do with finance. That must be settled with the Admiralty. A week later he was in khaki and a week later he was at the front.

I went back to the Commodore and told him what had been arranged. He approved.

'How long will it be before you are able to take in the patients? There is urgent need of haste.'

I thought for a moment.

'I guarantee the hospital will be ready for the patients in forty-eight hours if you can let me have men enough.'

'You can have as many men as you want. But don't promise more than is possible. I am trusting to you.'

'I shan't let you down, Sir.'

'How many men do you want?'

'500, and 10 petty officers.'

'You shall have them. At what time?'

'6.30 tomorrow morning, Sir.'

'But the twenty-four hours you gave the parson won't be up by that time.'

'Oh, he won't worry; he wants to help.'

Back to the Welcome. to plan out the next morning's work. I found the parson sitting with a dazed look on his face, and told him about the new arrangements. His answer was characteristic. 'Don't apologise. I've been wondering ever since you left why I wasn't bundled into the street straightaway and my hat thrown after me.'

The Welcome Sailors' Rest was a very large four-storied building opening directly on to the street and had depended for its existence on the Admiralty regulations which prohibited a sailor from returning to his ship between the hours of 10 p.m. and 7 a.m. Whether carousing or amusing himself innocently it is unlikely that a man will shorten his precious hours of leave by keeping such early hours, and the result was that the men had nowhere to sleep except brothels and police cells until various philanthropic people, headed by Miss Weston, came to the rescue with their Sailors' Homes. They filled a want which a more reasonable attitude on the part of the Admiralty would have prevented arising. In these homes the belated blue-jacket could get refreshment and a bed at practically any hour of the night, and of course full advantage was taken of them.

On the ground floor in the Welcome there was a large refreshment room with a long coffee bar in front and kitchens and domestic quarters behind. Each of the three upper floors consisted chiefly of an enormous hall on the floor of which had been laid out about 100 cubicles. The height of the room was about 15 feet and the walls of the cubicles 7 feet, the roof being open except for a strong wire netting spread over it. The walls of the cubicles were made of bamboo and plaster sheets about two inches thick, tongued and grooved into one another. In the cubicle there was room for a man to stand whilst dressing beside the narrow bed. The first thing to do was to knock all these cubicles down with the exception of some I wanted to retain for my sick berth staff. Besides these large rooms with the cubicles there were several smaller rooms and I made a mental note of their ultimate use as sisters' rooms, operating theatre, dispensary, etc. The parson's office I put down as my own room, and while he sat and gazed at me I ordered a new bed to be put up, and some blankets, pillows and sheets bought. I told him I was going to sleep there that night.

I telephoned to the barracks for my servant to pack my kit bag with my night gear and a few shirts and things and bring it up to me. The parson finally left for home, remarking as he went that I had the queerest notion of what twenty-four hours' notice meant, of any man he had ever come across.

I didn't sleep much. There was too much to think about and plan. At 6.30 the place was going to be invaded by 500 playful devils who were always out for a scrap, and it was my job to see that their bump of destruction had full play. The beds in the hostel were useless as they were so uncomfortable that only a drunken man could have slept in them, whilst the mattresses were soaked in urine, and stinking. It had been arranged with the parson that all his gear would be stored and I had to see that the necessary lorries were outside the hostel first thing in the morning. Then, just when the working party would be falling in to march off from the barracks, I remembered I had not ordered any demolition tools. A telephone message was just in time to remedy the oversight before they left.

Shortly afterwards I was wakened from an uneasy doze by the tramp of feet in the street outside and the order 'Halt! Front!' from a strident voice. Looking out from the window the street seemed to be filled with men, and at one end of the line I could see the lorries which were waiting to remove the discarded furniture. Luckily the Commander had sent a warrant officer in command of the party and he came up to the office and reported. 'Working party correct, Sir.' The warrant officers are a tower of strength to the Navy and this one was no exception to the rule. In ten minutes he had grasped what my scheme was, picked out and remedied the weak bits, and, having divided his party up so that all three floors were tackled simultaneously, he let loose the crowd on the removal of the furniture. That took about an hour, which was more than my W.O. had allowed for; but the staircases though very wide and easy were hardly wide enough to prevent collisions between ascending and descending men who were handling bulky pieces of furniture. As such collisions not only stopped the steady stream of traffic but offered opportunities for a joyous scrap the W.O. finally stopped the proceedings for a few minutes and told the men that any offenders would be returned to barracks at once. He must have managed to instil the idea that the work they were employed upon was one glorious bit of fun, because the men looked on his warning as a threat and the interruptions ceased.

Once the furniture was out the demolition of the cubicles was started, and there was no doubt that this was real fun for the men. The W.O. started a competition as to which room would be the first to be cleared, and with sledge hammers, crowbars, and shovels working fast and furiously the din and dust were appalling. The men not employed in demolition were told off to remove the rubbish down the stairs and heap it in a back yard whence it was subsequently removed by our barrack lorries.

Whilst the W.O. was in charge I was only in the way, so I went back to my office to arrange for the constructive work necessary. Luckily for me I had been a medical officer in the Dockyard a few years previously and I got on the telephone to tell an officer from the Works department and another from the Electrical Engineer's office that if they loved me or wanted to win the War they were to come up to the Welcome as soon as possible. Both listened to my requirements, which were staggering, and grinned like anything when I said they could begin that evening but must be finished by the next evening. The Works officer said I was expecting a week's work in one day but that he thought it could be done in relays of shifts. The electrical engineer said nothing, but with a stubby pencil on the back of an Admiralty envelope he was calculating the length of wire, switches, lights, and other requirements. We had no washing arrangements worth speaking of, and sinks, lavatories, wash hand basins, and a bath for the sisters' quarters had to be supplied and fitted. Whilst we argued and calculated, the shrieks of delight from the demolishers and the crashing of the bulkheads make speech almost impossible. But I told them the place would be ready for their workmen by 5 p.m. and somehow or other managed to get them to believe me.

The Works department official was the only one to drop a pebble into the pool of our perfect accord.

'Who is going to authorise all this expenditure?' said he.

I had already done things which in the ordinary Admiralty routine of 'approvals' and 'for further remarks' would have taken about a couple of years, and wasn't prepared to boggle at further commitments. At the back of my mind I hoped that the intense loyalty of the Commodore to his junior officers would prevent my head being submerged even although I was already in it up to the neck. So I said I would authorise it under the wide terms of my instructions, and then turned to the electrical engineer. That gentleman lit a cigarette, stuffed the stubby pencil into his waistcoat pocket, assured me 'We'll wangle it somehow,' and departed. I told the Works officer that the equipment of the operating theatre and the sisters' quarters could be delayed a few days if necessary, and he too left.

It was fairly certain that the groundwork of the hospital would be completed within the specified time, but the equipment was going to be a difficulty. The Naval Hospital could spare sufficient medical stores, bedding and a small supply of bed linen; but they were woefully short of beds, and could only let me have a small number. This had to be remedied somehow, so I went to a large firm of house furnishers in the district and asked whether they had any single beds for sale.

The manager took me to their stores and dilated in a pleasant salesmanlike fashion on the comfort and quality of his goods. He thought I wanted two or three for my own use, but I waited until he had given me the prices, and when he had finished I got up.

'That's quite satisfactory; I shall take the lot. Send them to the Welcome Sailors' Home not later than 5 o'clock tomorrow afternoon.'

The manager stared and stuttered.

'But it is ridiculous! I couldn't let you have the lot.'

'Why not?'

'Well, you see; we have many other customers to consider. I must have some left for them. Of course I might let you have half the number.'

Half the number was no use as the lot only just completed my essential requirements. I slowly pulled on my gloves, picked up my silver knobbed malacca, looked at him for a moment and, sick with anxiety but prepared to bluff for all I was worth, said as slowly and detachedly as I could: 'You know, these are extraordinary times and it would be of little value to your firm if we were compelled to exercise some of the extraordinary powers entrusted to us.'

He had not been prepared for the underlying threat in my words, which hit him fairly and squarely between the eyes. The salesman attitude disappeared and he was all eagerness to remove the impression he had given. 'Ah, yes. Yes. Of course. You shall have them, and I will see that they are delivered up to time. War necessity, of course!' And then he attempted to jest. 'Well, well! At any rate I suppose we shall get war prices for them.'

But I was beyond jesting. 'You will get the prices quoted to me, subject to the usual Admiralty discount for contracts.'

Back in the Home the work of demolition had been completed and the working party were busy sweeping up and cleaning, preparatory to handing over to the painters and distemperers. On my arrival I was told that a lady was waiting to see me, and sitting on the edge of a chair in the office I found a stout, elderly, plain looking woman evidently belonging to the better working class. As if repeating a lesson in an elementary school she began: 'I am the president of the Guild of British Women Workers and at a meeting to-day we agreed to adopt your hospital and help you by supplying any linen you might need.'

'But how did your Guild know about this Hospital? We haven't been here for twenty-four hours yet.'

'My husband heard a talk about it last night so I came down this morning to see if it was true. Then I called the meeting. I've just come from it.'

I had been pestered by useless cranks and idle offers of help all day and thought confound this Guild and its pettifogging ideas of help.

'What can you do for us at once?'

She enumerated about enough articles to equip four beds.

I meant to stagger her by saying what was really needed, believing that when I had told her she would fade away and leave me to get on with the work. So after referring to the lists that had been made up during the night I turned to her and said:

'What I urgently require is 1,000 sheets, 1,000 pillow slips and 500 towels.'

She blinked and shifted a bit on the edge of her chair.

'How long can you give us to get them ready for you?'

She sat still, stolid and unmoved; but there was no doubt she meant to do the work and I felt thoroughly uncomfortable and ashamed of my first estimate of her character.

'Do you really think you can do it? It will take a great load of anxiety off my mind if you can.'

'It will take a little time, Sir. Not that we mind working hard. But we are all poor people. And our subscriptions –'

I broke in at this. 'I shall give you an order for the cotton, the threads, needles and anything else you may require. Your responsibility will be confined to the work of making the articles up. And I don't want to hurry you but I should like half of them in a week.'

She rose to go. 'We can manage the work, Sir.'

'I should like you to tell your Guild from me how grateful I am for their help.'

'It's nothing, Sir. It's all we can do for our men.'

The work of the plumbers, the carpenters, the painters and the electricians for the next twenty-four hours was a holy calm compared with the racket of the demolition. The next thing to be arranged for was the victualling, and this required an expert. At my request a paymaster was sent up to discuss the details, and an officer who had been called up after retiring a few years before, appeared. He had been employed in a stockbroker's office so that in addition to a perfect knowledge of his job he was accustomed to quick decisions. Also, having no future service career to ruin, he looked only for efficiency and was prepared to work with that object in view in spite of the King's Regulations and Admiralty Instructions. He went over all the various financial aspects of the venture and straightened them out, dropped the letter from the parson demanding £60 a week as rent of the house into the waste paper basket, asked what numbers I proposed should be fed, interviewed the civilian cooks and attendants, condemned all the Home cooking gear and drew new from the Depot, and left me feeling giddy and breathless. The job was child's play he thought, and he was going back to the barracks to see whether he couldn't be given something more to do.

Late that night I rang up the barracks, reported that the hospital would be ready for the reception of the patients by 11.30, and that they would be supplied with dinner on arrival. I asked that the sick berth staff should report at 6 in the morning so as to get the beds fixed up and have their duties allotted to them, and asked that a steward C.P.O. whom I knew well should be sent in charge of the sick berth staff and to act as my secretary. In a naval hospital the paper work is like a snowball rolling downhill.

The patients arrived and everything was ready for them. After making the dinner rounds and hearing the usual 'Correct, Sir' I went to my room, sat down in front of my desk, put my head on my arms and had the first real sleep I had had for three days.

So far the work had been done to time, but it was a long way from being the smooth-running organisation that was expected. The chief difficulty was that none of our usually highly trained sick berth staff were available and their places had to be taken by a very new detachment of St. John's Ambulance men whose knowledge was confined to scrappy

First Aid Work. Also they were Lancashire lads with not the faintest idea of discipline. It was useless and dangerous to leave them in charge of seriously ill men without trained supervision, so I requested that four nursing sisters should be appointed to the hospital as soon as their accommodation was ready for them. This was agreed to and four very good temporary nurses arrived. I was not prepared to compete with all four of them so the senior was chosen as Matron, and then they scrapped happily amongst themselves.

The Matron was excellent, but she got me into trouble once. A very senior officer and a very great man had been brought back from his retirement and given the appointment of Inspecting Officer of Auxiliary Hospitals. He was a man I liked and admired very much, especially since the day when, up at the Admiralty, he had thrown a Quarterly Navy List at my head, because I had proved a contentious point from it. As the aforesaid King's Regulations and Admiralty Instructions do not provide for the procedure to be adopted on such occasions I was at a loss what to do; but, pending the decision of a superior authority, I did the best I could and picked up the battered volume, which had missed me and crashed into a corner of the room. With a wary eye on his apoplectic face I put the book down on a table well away from him. His apology was perfect and accepted in the spirit with which it was given. Put it down here! he said, indicating with his finger a place on his desk where it was within easy reach. Evidently the breeze was over, and we became good friends.

As Inspecting Officer he came down and visited my hospital, and after the usual routine was over came into my office to do some paper work. He had a very harsh Aberdeen accent, and he was late for his lunch.

'What do you mean by writing to me and saying that the nurses' accommodation was ready for their reception when it wasn't?'

'But it was, Sir.'

'It wasn't, I tell you! You've just sent me up a requisition for a hearth rug for the nurses' sitting room. That proves it wasn't ready, doesn't it?'

'I'm sorry, Sir. I never thought about the hearth rug when I reported the accommodation was ready.'

'A man of your sense ought to have known that the only use a woman has for a fire is to sit on the hearth rug in front of it.'

Somehow I felt I had failed him and all because that confounded Matron had told me she thought the room would look cosier with a rug. How was I to know that it was an essential part of the seating accommodation?

The St. John's Ambulance men were very difficult to handle. They hadn't the least conception of discipline, resented anything that savoured in the least of an order, and were only controlled by their elderly meek sergeant by appeals to their better feelings and what he would report about them when he got home. At first they were dressed in their own rig which included a white shoulder strap supporting a white pouch in which they kept their pipes, tobacco, and letters from their best girls. The Admiralty order came out that their own uniform was to be discarded and they were to be dressed in the uniform of the naval sick berth staff. They didn't mind the clothing but they strongly objected to leaving off this white belt, and again and again I had to dismiss the liberty men and stop their leave until they were properly dressed. One evening the C.P.O. reported that the liberty men were ready for inspection and on going round them I found one man, who had been especially obnoxious, still wearing this belt. I told him to fall out at once, go back to his quarters and report himself when he was properly dressed.

The C.P.O. repeated my orders. 'So-and-so fall out; report yourself when properly dressed. Liberty men! Right turn! Dismiss!'

A TEMPORARY HOSPITAL

Not a man moved. Evidently a trial of strength had been arranged.

I went up to the misclad one. 'Did you not hear my order just now? You are to return to your quarters and report when you are properly dressed.'

The man looked doggedly at the rank marks on my sleeves. 'If only you'd take that jacket off I'd teach you not to treat men as if they were machines!'

It was a quandary. There were several things that could be done and the most obvious was to ring up the barracks and ask for a file of marines to come up and take the man away under arrest. But I was not inclined to push my troubles on to other people's shoulders and the effect on the others would have been to make them sympathise with the offender and consider him harshly used.

So after doing some quick thinking I said:

'If you will meet me on the Dorland Banks after rounds tonight I don't think you will find my jacket interfering with my movements much. But you must come properly dressed or you will be arrested by the picket and I shall be disappointed.'

'Oh, I'll be there,' he said as he fell out.

The order to dismiss was obeyed this time and I have no doubt most of them made straight for the Dorland Banks.

A little later the C.P.O. reported that the man had put in a request to see me, and he was brought before me at once. He looked sheepish and ill-atease. His sergeant, who of course came with him, looked worried to death.

'I've been told you're a bit of a bruiser, Sir.'

'What about it?'

'I'm no' frightened of you, Sir.'

'Well, I am of you. You might give me a black eye and I'd look a funny sight going round the wards.'

The ghost of a smile flickered across his face. 'I just wanted to tell you that you can do what you like with me, but whatever you do I'm sorry I spoke to you the way I did.' The apology did not come easily but it was heartfelt.

I got up and held out my hand. 'I'm sorry I'm not allowed to let you go about dressed just as you please, but we ought to be good friends after this.'

That was the end of these troubles. Very soon the Ambulance men settled down to their work and the strange life they were leading. What they lacked in skill and knowledge they soon made up by their eagerness and willingness to learn. When I left I could not have wished for a better crowd.

Of course the medical work was too much for a single hand, and two junior medical officers were detailed for duty in the hospital. As there was no accommodation for them at the Welcome they slept and fed in the barracks mess. One of their duties was to do the evening round at 8.45 p.m., and one of them, an Irishman newly joined, was always late. I remonstrated with him again and again, but he had all the Irishman's disregard for time and a wholehearted belief in the efficacy of excuses. On one occasion, as he had not arrived by 9 o'clock I did the rounds myself, so that the hospital might settle down for the night. A few minutes later he turned up panting and breathless and started a long-winded story of how he had been late for dinner and after that had stayed yarning in the smoking room until it was later than he thought, so that he had had to run all the way to arrive at the time he did. I had heard all this sort of thing before and took a serious view of it and told him that I must ask for another officer to replace him. 'You know, I told him, there were 180 patients, there were 30 of the sick berth staff, there were 4 sisters, and all the lighting of the hospital held up waiting for your arrival. 'Yes, yes,' he said, his voice full of contrition; 'and there was me running like a hound and sweating like a pig. Yes, sweating like a pig, I was!'

Poor boy, I have often wondered whether the D.S.O. he won when medical officer of the *Clyde* at Gallipoli compensated for the limp which he will carry to the end of his days.

As the hospital opened directly on to the street by several doors communicating with the refreshment bar on the ground floor there were numberless loafers constantly butting in either out of curiosity or with some ill defined ideas of assisting. At first it was difficult to distinguish them from various people who had some excuse for their entry. But I thought things like this had gone far enough when, during the inspection of the St. John's people one morning, the tail of the line was occupied by an elderly man whom I had seen at odds and ends of times doing small jobs in various parts of the building. He was well over sixty but active and intelligent looking, dressed in civilian trousers, waistcoat and a clean white linen jacket. The jacket was open displaying a long row of medals pinned across the left breast of his waistcoat – an unusual sight in the days when medals were rare. As several people had been taken on I presumed he was one of the civilian helpers and hitherto not paid much attention to him. But it was certain he had no business falling in with the staff, so when the end of the line was reached I asked him:

'What are you doing here?'

'Just falling in, Sir.'

'I can see that. But what's your job?'

'Haven't any particular job, Sir.'

'Then what are you?'

'Just a willing 'elper, Sir.'

'Have you been in any of the services?'

'No, Sir.'

I ran my finger under his row of medals and recognised the South African Medal and our own Long Service and Good Conduct one. The ribbons were on the wrong medals. The rest of the decorations were unknown to me and appeared to be chiefly shooting trophies.

'Then how did you get these?'

'Just presents from friends, Sir.'

'Well, you can't do this sort of thing. Clear out!'

'Yes, Sir.'

The next morning it chanced that I went to my office at a time when I was usually working in the wards. Our friend was there busy with a dustpan and brush. He stopped when I came in and stood to attention.

'I thought I had told you already to clear out.'

'Yes, Sir.'

'Well, clear out!'

'And come back and finish when you've gone, Sir?'

'No! clear out altogether!'

'Yes, Sir.'

The next time I saw him was about half an hour later. He was sweeping the stairs. They badly needed it. Later on about 4 o'clock when sitting at my desk he appeared again, this time with a neatly arranged tea tray which he put down at my elbow. It was the first decently served cup of tea I had seen for nearly a month.

He turned to go, but I stopped him.

'Look here, my friend, our conversation is getting monotonous. I'm tired of saying " Get out" and hearing you say "Yes, Sir".'

'Yes, Sir.'

'Oh, shut up!'

'Yes, Sir.'

The parable of the unjust judge and the importunate widow must have been his favourite reading and he had put me in the position of the unjust judge. It was time to make terms with him.

'Look here! What's your game?'

(A trifle hurt): 'Haven't any game, Sir.'

'Do you want to be taken on the civilian staff?'

'No, Sir.' It was the first 'No' I had heard from him and the sound was refreshing.

'You can be enrolled on the civilian staff and receive pay like the rest.'

'Don't want any pay, Sir.'

'Then what do you want?'

'Only to be allowed to be a willing 'elper, Sir.'

Short of physical violence there seemed to be no method of kicking him out, and even then I believe he would have hobbled back on crutches. So he was allowed to remain. He refused his name and address, and the only reward he ever got for devotion to endless small duties was his midday dinner and tea in the hospital. Even in the best organised establishment there are plenty of jobs which an odd man can carry out and he had a knack of picking them up and making them his own. Before I left he had made himself indispensable.

Towards the end of my time I was astonished to receive a message from a local pub that one of the barmaids wished to speak to me, at once if possible; it was a well-known lounging place for the junior naval officers and was owned by a German, though whether he was naturalised or not I do not know. I had never been in the place in my life and my attraction for barmaids is small so it was impossible to understand the urgency of the message; but as it was 7 o'clock in the evening there was nothing to hinder me obeying the call at once. I guessed it might concern a medical officer who was making an ass of himself.

When I entered the lounge I found it crowded, and there was an awkward hush for a moment as all the youngsters who were in uniform recognised the unusual sign of the presence of a senior officer. Behind the bar were several young women very much bedizened and bedight, and all with a men of rollicking friendliness. The air was putrid with gin and tobacco smoke. As I hesitated for a moment one of the girls, whom my manse forebears would have characterised as a 'hussy', shouted out to me: 'Hullo, doctor; glad to see you back,' and I stepped forward to her end of the bar, guessing that she was the one who had sent for me. She held out her hand in a most friendly fashion, shook mine heartily and whispered: 'Order something, will you, and then we can talk'. I had no money in my pocket except a 10s. treasury note, with which I paid for the drink I ordered. Later investigation showed me that she had handed me 10s. in silver, although I did not notice it at the time. Whilst getting the drink her conversation indicated that we had been on loving terms for years, to my intense embarrassment and the sniggering amusement of the youngsters, few of whom belonged to the regular service. With a sweep of her arm she placed the drink at one end of the bar and called out, 'Now we can have a talk just like old times', leant across the bar until her peroxide hair was almost brushing my grizzled pow, put out her hand and stroked affectionately the rank marks on my sleeve which was resting on the marble top. Her face was alluring and entirely friendly but utterly failed to match the seriousness of her words.

'These are the rank marks of a medical officer, aren't they?' and again she stroked my sleeve.

'What about it?' My looks and voice were forbidding.

'Laugh and make love to me. I don't want somebody here to suspect anything.'

This was interesting and I did my best to get my rugged features to comply with the unaccustomed requirement.

She then spoke quickly and seriously. 'Don't look round, but there's a man dressed as a lieutenant sitting at a table over in the corner on your right. He is in here every night standing drinks all round and pumping these boys for all he's worth.

He told us girls he was a newly joined surgeon waiting for a job, and we don't know naval uniforms very well so I said I'd find out. I hope you didn't mind me sending for you. You were the only one near enough to catch him when he was in here.' Her expression was the 'Kiss me quick or I'll die' one.

I had stolen a glance at the man indicated. He was undoubtedly taking a deeper interest in us than I thought the circumstances warranted. 'He's not a surgeon at any rate, whatever his rank in the Service may be. What is he up to?'

The amazing young woman! She drew back suddenly and held the flat of her hand towards me as if I had made an effort at kissing her. Then she shook her golden curls, put her head forward and whispered in my ear so that any observer could have sworn an assignation was being arranged.

'I think he's a spy!'

Of course Chatham was full of rumours of spies at the time and there was no doubt it was an ideal place for getting information. If anything was to be done it had to be done quickly.

'How long will he stay here?'

'He generally stops till closing time. He's always standing drinks but he hardly drinks anything himself.'

'What does he call himself?'

She told me.

'All right; leave it to me.'

She nodded happily. To everyone around the assignation was proceeding smoothly. I looked at her carefully, and behind the make-up, the golden hair, and the black silk dress designed to accent the attractive figure, I saw something that made me raise my uniform cap as I said goodnight. I never saw her again. A message to the barracks and an hour later the supposed spy was under arrest. With that he disappeared from my ken.

Gradually things settled down. The work was carried along by its own momentum and one was able to sleep at night to the accompaniment of marching feet and the singing of 'Tipperary' as the men of Kitchener's army marched past my window on their way from the railway station to the camp on the Chatham lines. All night long they marched and sang, just as they marched and sang to the end. There were doings on the waters which stirred the soul of every sailor man still tied to the solid earth and made him long to be playing his part too, If you have the sea in your blood you will turn to it always, whether in war or in peace, and find no ease for your longing until you can see the horizon on every side, speak the speech of sailor men, and mix with those who do business on the Great Waters.

Risk? Yes. That risk was borne in on us on one September morning when the crowds of wailing women strove round the steps of the Town Hall in Chatham in order to read the list of casualties from the *Aboukir*, *Cressy* and *Hogue*. Although nearly 400 yards away I had to shut the hospital windows to keep the sound of them from my patients' ears.

The comparative inaction of shore work and the stifling security of stone walls had become intolerably oppressive. It was time to be going.

Chapter III
Our Ship

The Medical Director General had completed his inspection of the temporary hospital which I had been ordered to organise during the first few weeks of the War. He was not a man given to words of approval, but the absence of fierce criticism was just as significant of satisfaction, and with some trepidation I told him I had a request to make.

'What is it?'

'I want to be sent to sea, Sir.'

'Some medical officers would be thankful for a safe shore billet like this.'

I made no answer. It was no concern of mine what the aspirations of other men might be. He considered for a little.

'When can you turn over?'

'I should want twenty-four hours to muster stores, Sir.'

'You will have the best ship I can give you.'

Nothing more was said. Two days afterwards I was told that my relief had been appointed and that, when the muster of stores was completed, I was to proceed to Clydebank to take medical charge of a newly completed battle cruiser. She had a skeleton crew on board and would be regularly commissioned with a full crew three or four days after my arrival. The exact date was of course a secret, so I was not altogether surprised to be told by my Chief Sick Berth Steward in the Hospital that it was to be on the 3rd October.

My relief duly turned up, inspected with me the hospital wards with their 180 patients, the rows of St. John's

Ambulance men who had been called up for the War, the temporary nursing sisters, the domestic staff who had been taken over with the establishment which had been previously used as a Sailors' Home, and the sprinkling of Naval ratings who formed the backbone of the whole. He expressed himself as satisfied and the next evening found me in the train for Glasgow. Whilst passing through London it was my duty to call on the Director General and I did so. On entering his room it was impossible to assume I was welcome, but at least he didn't throw me out.

'What do you want?'

'To thank you for my appointment, Sir, and to report myself in accordance with the instructions.'

'Gir-r-r!'

Conversation seemed difficult. His little piercing blue eyes behind bushy grey eyebrows glared threateningly at me.

'I am very old for my seniority, Sir. I was late in joining the Service.'

'What do you want?' he snapped.

Only this, Sir. If we should be in action in this ship I might get specially promoted. Otherwise I shall have to retire for age.'

'Plenty better men have done so.'

I had shot my bolt and got up. But he motioned me to sit down again.

'I promise you that if you do well, your special circumstances will be considered.'

Early next morning on arrival in Glasgow I went to the Station Hotel and booked a room. Stupidly enough I left my pocket-book with a lot of money in it on the dressing table while I went to have a bath. It was gone on my return and the affair was at once reported to a black clad lady who sat in the office. She was not at all impressed.

'Did you look everywhere for the money?'

'Yes. I have told you the money was in my pocket-book on the dressing table when I went to my bath, and the book and money were gone on my return.'

'Did you lock the door of your room?'

'Yes, and I opened it with my key when I came back.'

'Well, all I can tell you is that a commercial gentleman in that room made. the same complaint last week and when we searched the room the money was found at the back of a picture where he had put it when he was drunk. Go back and look again.'

And that was all I ever heard about my lost pocket-book. Luckily I had enough loose change to pay my bill, and my railway pass took me down to Clydebank station with my luggage. There seemed to be an awful lot of the latter, although in accordance with Admiralty orders all the gewgaws of Naval life had been eliminated, and the services of a porter were necessary to take the gear to the ship. No porter was to be found, as the usual man had been called up, and after considerable searching a friendly Scot with a barrow intimated his willingness to assist. We got the gear on board, stowed it for the time being in the flat outside my cabin, and then I handed my friend two half-crowns. He looked at them in his palm for a bit, transferred his attention to me, eyed the coins again, ejaculated 'Losh me!' and made off up the companion ladder as fast as he could travel. Later that day whilst standing at the gate of the dockyard he came up to me showing every evidence of having tested the purchasing power of his gratuity. 'Eh man! That was a fine tip ye gied me this morning. Come awa down the road a bit and I'll stand ye a drink.' It was explained that the offer was a tempting one but that my being in uniform made things a bit difficult. 'Oh aye! I ken! They navy people are gey hard on you folk. Nae liberty ava!' The apostle of liberty lurched off down the street, doubtlessly congratulating himself that he had been able to do the right thing at so little expense.

The enormous grey mass of the largest, fastest, and most powerful battle cruiser in the world lay alongside the fitting out jetty in John Brown's dockyard. From the brow amidships which connected her with the shore her bows stretched in the distance apparently into the middle of the yard, whilst aft her stern was well into the waters of the muddy Clyde. Speed and beauty were welded into every line of her. Here indeed was a ship! The highest ideals of grace and power had taken form at the bidding of the artist's brain of her designer. Wherever she went she satisfied the eye of the sailorman and I have known them to pull miles just that the sweetness of her lines might delight their eyes. She was the last warship built to satisfy the sailors' ideas of what a ship should be like, and nobly she fulfilled that ideal. Beside any others she made them look like floating factories. No man who ever served in her fails to recollect her beauty with pride and thankfulness.

But on board! Wherever there was foothold for two men three seemed to be making an effort at balancing. Her completion had been hastened, as on her presence depended the margin of superiority of the British battle cruisers over the German. Right nobly the builders had answered to the call for haste. Men drilling, men hammering, men tapping, men painting, men furnishing, men rigging. Everywhere there were men. Below, in the dimly lit depths of the engine room and stokeholds, in every compartment and crevice you stumbled against men. And over all huge cranes were slinging stores on board to fall amongst the working parties and add to the apparent confusion. In my small cabin when I tried to enter it I found one man wiring the electric leads, another painting, and a third fitting a telephone and a buzzer. If there had been room for a fourth he would have been there. Only three days before the ship would commission, and then fifteen hundred men would be poured into her. Was the thing humanly possible? All my long years of naval service combined to shout to me, 'Absolutely impossible,' to be answered by the haggard Commander's assurance 'It will be!'

It was done! How, will be a mystery as long as life lasts. On the dank dreary morning of the 3rd October, 1914, fifteen hundred men, with bag, baggage and equipment, left the train which had brought them from Devonport, descended on the ship, jostled into their messes in spite of the caulkers, wiremen, painters, shipwrights and every conceivable class of dockyard workmen, chose their hammock hooks between which their beds would be slung, got the cooks of their messes to draw their rations, and by evening the whole ship had settled down in a fair degree of order.

When it came to turning in after a weary day a difficulty arose, the prospect of which had been worrying the Commander ever since he had joined the ship a month before. The peace time complement of the ship was nine hundred, and nearly six hundred more men had been allotted to bring the ship's company up to war strength. No effort had been made to find slinging accommodation for the extra hammocks, nor were the necessary bag racks for the kitbags fitted. Of course such trifles as racks for the' ditty-boxes' in which Jack keeps all his personal knick-knacks, mess tables and mess stools were also missing, and though you might cram extra men on to mess stools alongside the mess tables there is no way of hanging two hammocks from the same hooks. Space had to be found for these extra men somewhere, and this duty fell on the overburdened shoulders of the Commander, the work not being made any the easier by the fact that the ship was still being completed and night shifts of dockyard men were being worked.

When night came those who had hammock billets allotted to them turned in, whilst the remainder not on duty turned in as best they could on their hammocks laid out on the mess decks. I went to bed, but not for long. One of the newly joined had seen fit to attempt suicide by cutting his arteries at the wrists; but his anatomical knowledge was not equal to his intent. He turned out to be an elderly volunteer. With great trouble and much telephoning I found a hospital in Glasgow, and he was transferred there, to die shortly afterwards of acute mania.

Some twenty officers had joined the wardroom mess, bringing us up to our usual total of thirty-two. They were all sorts, R.N.R., R.N.V.R., retired officers called up, and of course the active service people. They were as fine a body of messmates as one could wish to have, all specially picked for the ship, keen and competent.

They had had one amusing experience on the way up. During the night their train had stopped in the station of a midland town. The officers in one compartment were doing their best to sleep when the door was flung open by an irate female.

'There's some soldiers outside on the platform here insulting me. Come out and bash them!'

The Senior Officer tried to explain.

'We're not soldiers, we're Royal Navy. We can't interfere. Get hold of the military picket.'

'That's nothing to do with me. Come out at once, I tell you, and bash them. Will you see a lady insulted and do nothing?'

'I tell you it's none of our business.'

'Do you mean to tell me you won't bash them?'

'No, of course not.'

'Then what do you think we pay you for.'

The movement of the train obviated the need for a reply to this conundrum.

Like all ships commissioned after the outbreak of war our ship's company at first was painfully inefficient. Perhaps two-thirds were regular service ratings and to them a new ship was merely a question of a few days in which to find their way about. But the best of the reserves and volunteers had been called up at the beginning of the war and allotted to ships. Those sent to us were the sweepings of the recruiting offices. Good men as they proved to be, once the service had taken hold of them and moulded them into her ways, at the beginning they were a danger and a constant source of anxiety. The mere complexity of the ship, especially below decks, completely mazed them, and it was a common thing to find men walking aft when they thought they were going forward, and believing they were on the starboard side when they were on the port. During the first morning the wardroom Corporal of servants was aghast at finding a group of newly enlisted Scotch stokers sitting on the settees in the wardroom. One of them, when he came up to ask them to leave, was quite friendly. 'They ships are no so bad once you get downstairs; but of course they're no a patch on the Clyde steamers for comfort. This is the bar, I suppose.' The horrified marine had the greatest of difficulty in getting them to believe they were sitting in the officers' quarters. It was only when he passed a message for some marines to come and turn them out that they left with an ill grace.

Completion was still a will-o'-the-wisp when we pushed out of our berth into the Clyde and made our officially secret departure to the heartening huzzas of thousands of excursionists lining the banks of the river to see the largest vessel ever built on the Clyde. Somehow our gigantic mass was pulled and pushed and buffeted into midstream at the hour of high water, and we anchored without mishap at the Tail of the Bank. There we began the job of coaling ship before making the passage to Plymouth.

That coal ship! Usually it is done by the officers and men, dressed in their oldest clothing, to the tune of rattling Temperleys, thuds of coal bags on the deck, whirring of trolleys and shouts of laughter from semi-demented white-eyed kaffirs attempting to beat a record. With a crew, half of whom did not know the ship and the other half never having seen a coaling in their lives, the whole evolution was a nightmare of frustrated effort. A smart crew should be able to coal ship at the rate of 350–400 tons an hour, but our best never approached the half of that amount, and after nearly forty-eight hours the Engineer Commander reported that we were burning the stuff even faster than we could take it in. There was no use going on.

However, we had enough coal to take us to Plymouth, and if that gave out we could burn oil fuel, which a tanker had been pumping into us. Besides our own fifteen hundred on board there was a swarm of dockyard men still busy completing. There were supposed to be about two thousand of them and they were to remain until we arrived at Plymouth. So with thirty-five hundred men we made another secret departure, and all Greenock, Gourock and the various little towns on the shores of the Firth turned out in their thousands to wish us God-speed. And a German minelayer, knowing of our departure and expecting us to avoid the narrow St. George's Channel as a death trap, obligingly laid some mines for us off Tory Island. But we went through the Channel and the mines got the *Audacious* instead. The Admiralty handling of that affair blackened our faces for ever as a truthful people and bore its own bitter fruit in the reception of the plain straightforward account of the battle of Jutland two years afterwards.

We arrived at Plymouth and added another worry to the Port Authorities, who were getting ready for the arrival of the first contingent of the Canadian troops. The dock was not ready for us so we could not go up the Hamoaze, and to lie in the unprotected Sound at night-time would be to offer an easy prey to a submarine. This could not be risked; we should be safer at sea. So out into the Channel at nightfall we went, to cruise up and down at 15 knots until daylight came and we could come in again.

But other ships were in the Channel as well, and at midnight the alarm went in my cabin. I was up and dressed like lightning.

'What's the flap now?'

'Oh, nothing; just run into the French destroyer patrol and they've made the private signal.'

'Well, answer it.'

'We can't find the answer. Somebody has slipped up somewhere.'

'Oh, let's run away, then.'

'Can't; we've only got steam for fifteen knots and it will take a couple of hours to work up to thirty-three, and in the meantime they may slip a mouldy into us.'

'Well, fight the beggars.'

'We haven't got any ammunition.'

So the conversation was bandied about whilst we waited. The Frenchmen held their hands long enough for the secret signal to be found and all was well. The French destroyer Commander said afterwards that they were horribly alarmed when they saw us looming through the darkness, but they speedily recognised us and guessed the reason for the delay in answering them. 'Newly commissioned ship' explains a lot to a seaman. Still, I like to think of those twenty torpedo tubes trained on our bilge and only held in leash by the conviction of the Commander that we looked more like a British ship than a German one. Success in an action between us would have depended entirely on which ship got its blow in first,

By and by we were dry docked, coaled, oiled, provisioned, watered, ammunitioned and got rid of our dockyard ratings. The Canadian contingent came in and for one I was glad to see them, as a sister whom I had not seen for years was serving as a nurse on board the *Franconia*. It was a strange meeting.

Meanwhile as medical officer I was sorely worried. In every shipbuilding contract there is always a clause that the ship is to be thoroughly cleaned before she is accepted by the Admiralty. The necessity for this clause is obvious to anyone who knows anything about the habits of the dockyard matey, especially in the northern civil yards. I yield to none in my admiration for him as a craftsman, but as a human being his sanitary habits have literally and on many occasions made me sick. Instead of using the accommodation provided, any and every possible part of the ship had been used as a latrine, and the wing passages and compartments could only be entered wearing sea boots and oilskins, which had to be discarded and cleansed as soon as the compartment was left. There had been no time to insist on the clause mentioned, and the nuisance was going on right up to the day the men were discharged in Plymouth. The stench and filth were terrible, the ship was overcrowded, and sleeping and mess accommodation had not yet been arranged for the wartime complement. Everything that was possible was being done, but the ship was a fighting one before everything else, and other matters had to give place to the welding of her heterogeneous crew into an efficient fighting unit. The officers and men were all over-worked, one of them so much so that I have known him fall asleep if he stopped to lean up against a bulkhead. It would be a long time before the ship would be really sweet and clean.

Before joining the Fleet every newly commissioned ship in peace time is sent away by herself for a shake-down cruise. That usually lasts several months and not until then is she considered fit to vie with her squadron mates in evolutions and exercises. I knew that our shake-down would be reduced to the minimum or cut out altogether, but a short period by ourselves for gunnery and calibration was bound to be ordered, and it seemed likely that Berehaven would be chosen for this work and we should be there for a fortnight or so.

My opinion was that a cruise such as this in winter weather, with short daylight, rain and darkened ship, would tell on the health and spirits of the crew and render them more liable to suffer from the septic infection with which the ship dripped. The matter was discussed several times with the Captain, who agreed with all I put forward, and he promised to do his utmost to be allowed to take the ship to Tetuan Bay. There in the perfect Mediterranean weather the ship's company could live on deck the whole time, and the fresh air and sunlight would help to dry and sweeten the ship while she was being swilled from stem to stern.

The Captain made his representations and made them hard. The time came to leave Plymouth and we sailed under sealed orders which were only to be opened at a certain position. They were opened when the time came and the Captain sent for me.

'I'm sorry. Our orders are to proceed to Berehaven for our shake-down cruise and gun calibration.'

'Heaven help us,' I thought as I left the cuddy. In a month the ship was little better than a floating hospital, with an epidemic of virulent tonsillitis which caused several deaths.

About this time we heard with dismay that, in obedience to the clamour of the mob, the only First Lord who in our opinion was competent from his knowledge and love of the sea to handle our naval affairs and who possessed the complete confidence and affection of the whole Service to a degree equalled by none since the days of Nelson, had been dragged broken hearted from his appointment and replaced by the man who had destroyed the band of brotherhood of the Service. Great as Lord Fisher's claims were, his personal actions had destroyed all confidence and sureness. Even at the dinner table of a senior captain before the War when a guest had let fall a remark about the Bacon episode, which had been greeted with a stony silence, I have known the host glance nervously round the officers at his end of the table and say apologetically: 'I hope we are all friends here.' That remark was also received in silence. Every man there suspected the other of being a 'Fisher Spy'. Some years previously, whilst serving in a ship in the Mediterranean, the hero of the Falkland Islands action asked me for the loan of my *Blackwood* as he wished to read an anonymous article entitled 'Fool Gunnery in the Navy'. We could all guess who the writer was and there was no need to mention the name when the magazine was handed back with the remark 'That's the end of him all right!' The prophecy was very soon fulfilled.

The breed of the censor is a curious one and the story of the one who deleted 'The Captains and the Kings depart' from a reporter's account of a conference always seemed to typify the lot. I was never at a loss for plenty to say about them myself, and of course the irony of things turned me into a censor too. Officially some control had to be made over the vast correspondence which left the ship by every available post, and the Paymaster in Chief and I were appointed as Chief Censors, with power to drag in anyone we could induce to help us. As it was not unusual for over 1000 letters to leave the ship at a time, and we did not want to hang them up, one of our methods was to throw bundles of letters on the table after dinner and ask the others over their coffee to censor a few of them. This helped considerably, but often there was no help at all to lighten our labour of anything but love – although the correspondence was chiefly concerned with that subject.

But the duty was boredom beyond words. The average bluejacket had a stereotyped form of letter to his loved one, and a printed postcard, leaving a judicious amount of space for crosses, would have been equally enlightening as to the sender's sentiments. The Paymaster and I soon discovered that it was possible and a great saving of time to scan a letter so that not a single word of it could be understood and yet we would unfailingly pick up any statement which might be considered as of value to the enemy or contravening the regulations. In this way we habitually spent three and sometimes four hours a day in the most vacuous form of employment that can be imagined. The mistakes censored were entirely due to carelessness and we had to watch the officers' letters more carefully than any of the others.

One of the junior officers who, by virtue of his youth and undeniable good looks, carried on a catholic correspondence with divinities from Land's End to Kirkwall, particularly resented the censorship of his letters, and again and again insisted that he should be allowed to deliver his letters sealed and not open as the regulations demanded. He was told, of course, that we had no power to grant this privilege without his case going before the Captain for approval, but he was unwilling to do this.

One evening after dinner, whilst the whole mess was busy censoring, he tackled me on the subject, said he was an officer and a gentleman just as much as I was, that my letters were not censored, and if I could be trusted he didn't see why he shouldn't be.

The reply was that all my letters were censored by the Paymaster.

'And who censors his?'

'I do.'

'Well, all the same I call it a damned shame. There is no need to censor my letters. I'm not such a fool as to give anything away.'

As luck would have it, I had a batch of officers' letters in my pocket censored and sealed by myself before dinner and all ready for the post. I pulled them out, selected one and handed it to him.

'This is one of your letters, isn't it?'

'Yes. Why?'

'Open it and see.'

He ran a pencil under the flap, prised it up by rolling the pencil downwards, pulled out the letter and looked at the heading of his notepaper, where the censor's erasure stamp was plainly visible to the rest of the mess. He tossed the letter on the table, jumped up and fled hastily from the wardroom, followed by the jeers of the rest of the mess. In a forgetful moment he had headed his letter, after the pre-war fashion, with the name of the port at which we were lying, and this came under the heading of supplying information likely to be of value to the enemy and was a serious offence.

Despite all the censoring it could be circumvented by the simple process of posting a letter whilst ashore on the short periods of leave granted to us. This was forbidden and punishable if discovered, but there was no way of preventing it short of stripping and searching everyone who was going on shore leave.

Censoring the bluejackets' letters I once stumbled very badly. On holding an envelope up to the light I saw some writing under the postage stamp, and on removing it I found the letters SWALK. To make matters still worse a P.S. in the letter advised the fair recipient to look under the stamp. We were in the censor's office at the time so a messenger was ordered to fetch the writer, and an embarrassed looking young A.B. answered the summons. The offence of attempting to conceal correspondence under the stamp was explained to him and also he was told that he must let me know what these letters indicated. He got very red and refused to answer. The titters of the postmen and messengers ought to have warned me, but I blundered on.

'What do these letters mean?'

'It's only something we bluejackets send to our girls, Sir.'

'If you don't tell me at once what they mean you will be put in the rattle and appear before the Captain.'

'Sealed With A Loving Kiss,' was the answer. Dignity and censorship went by the board amidst howls of laughter from all the other occupants of the office, and blushing to the roots of his hair the A.B. was permitted to go. Neither he nor I heard the end of this incident for a long time afterwards. The favourite jibe at me was for an innocent looking young officer to say that he had heard the censorship was getting still more strict – they were even censoring the shapes of the crosses, and asking me for a copy of the approved pattern.

The ship remained at Berehaven for about a fortnight, going to sea. every morning for gunnery exercises and returning to the haven at night-time to anchor close under the island. We were giving ideal chances to an enterprising submarine if any such existed, and the thought was often present in the minds of the officers on board and the soldiers who were in charge of a small battery on the island.

One evening we had finished coaling for the day and the collier was still lashed alongside when about ten o'clock the alarm went and immediately afterwards 'Action Stations.' I was sitting reading in my cabin at the time and got up to go forward to my station with no further idea than that a drill routine was being carried out and grateful that it had not come when I was sound asleep in bed. To get forward I had to pass along a narrow dimly lit alleyway which ran between the engine room bulkheads and the wing compartments. Halfway along I saw ahead of me a confused mob of half-dressed men, and when I had got away from the constant noise of the turbo-generators I could hear an eerie yowling and mewing which reminded me of nothing so much as a cat fight. Pressing along rapidly to see what was the matter I suddenly found myself for the first time in my life face to face with panic. Apparently two bodies of men scrambling along in opposite directions and in an extremity of fear had met in the darkness of the narrow passage and, bereft of all reason and self control, were fighting to get past one another. If they had fought like men it would have been nothing; but they mewed and scratched at one another as if in a slow motion picture, whilst their white drawn faces and wildly staring eyes showed ghastly under the dimmed electric lights. Such is the infectivity of mob panic that for one horrible moment, which has taught me more about our weak human nature than I am ever likely to learn again, I felt impelled to join that fearsome fighting crowd, and with tooth and nail strive to reach my station. The reaction was almost instantaneous and I was once again my own man. Seizing hold of the nearest man, who turned round and wildly clawed at me, I forced him to one side, then another, then another, pushing those with their backs to me to the right and those facing me to the left. For one moment they got me down and I should have been seriously injured but for the fact that they had just tumbled out of their hammocks and none of them were wearing boots. As I got up again the men behind me recognised that I was an officer and even in their distraction the normal respect for a uniform made them stay at the side to which they had been pushed, but the remainder seemed hopelessly insane. Then, welcome sight! appeared at the far end of the mob an engineer lieutenant. He was a big powerful man and at one glance he took in what was happening; lowering his head he dashed in like a bull amongst them. In half a minute it seemed the panic was over and the men were passing one another easily in their respective directions. Shaken and shivering at the memory of my own dark moment of self revelation, I made my way to the Distributing Station.

My staff were already assembled and had made the usual preparations. They seemed a bit excited but were perfectly steady, and ready for anything that might come along. They told me that there was a persistent rumour we were being attacked by a submarine. This was interesting and I went outside the station to glean further news.

As soon as I got into the flats I met the Commander, who looked grave; so I asked: 'Would you mind letting me know if this is an exercise or the real thing?'

'It's the real thing all right', he said. 'We are being attacked by a submarine. Can't you hear the forts firing on shore?' I listened, and faintly through the thickness of our steel walls one could hear the dull boom of guns. I went back to my station.

Whether it was the real thing or not I do not know, and the question was never definitely settled. The forts ashore claimed to have driven off the submarine, which was attacking on the surface, and finally we all piped down. But whilst the excitement was at its height a comedy was being enacted on the upper deck. The Captain of the collier had no wish to intercept the torpedo meant for us, and the Captain of the man-of-war knew that as long as torpedoes run at 14 feet the collier, drawing 20 feet, was a sure shield to the vitals of his ship, especially as she was on the only side from which an attack could be launched. As soon as the forts began to fire the collier Captain rang up his engine room and ordered his hands to cast off the warps which secured him to the battle cruiser. The Naval Captain gave orders that the collier was to stay where she was. The collier refused and repeated his orders to cast off the warps. The Naval Captain threatened to shoot the first man who touched the warps and, as too often happens in a sinful world, force won. At any rate next morning the collier was still alongside. Both Captains were in the right. The first duty of a seaman is to ensure the safety of his ship.

The panic in the alleyway was the panic of undisciplined men. None of them were regular service ratings and some of them, roused suddenly from their sleep by the alarm, had heard the firing of the shore guns. The first and most important result of discipline is that it casts out fear by substituting the necessity for action in its place. In my early days I was discussing the question of discipline with a well-known Admiral who was also my senior officer. When asked what his definition was, he thought for a moment and then said, 'In my opinion discipline is intelligent obedience given to reasonable orders.' I have often considered this definition, and the more it is thought over, the more perfect it seems to be. It responsibility on both the commander and the commanded, and with this definition in mind I have no hesitation in saying that the discipline in His Majesty's Navy is of the highest possible order. It was good to see those same men who had panicked in November when we fought at the Dogger in January.

Chapter IV
Our Officers

On board a man-of-war and for naval service purposes generally, officers are divided into two great groups, executive and non-executive. Prior to the War the distinction made was combatant and non-combatant, but as mine, shell and torpedo refused to ratify this arrangement by giving preferential treatment, it has gradually fallen into disuse in favour of the grouping first indicated. During the War it became obvious that the old hard and fast distinctions between executive and non-executive officers could no longer be maintained, and as a first step the differences in uniform between the two branches were abolished, with the exception that the professional branches retained the strips of coloured cloth between the rings of gold lace on their sleeves. For Paymaster this was white, for Medical Officers red, for Engineers chocolate, and so on. The curl on the sleeve, formed by working the lace of the upper stripe into a circle, which had been long looked upon as the distinctive badge of the executive officer, was granted to all officers. The designations of the various nonexecutive branches seemed to have grown up any old how, and when the engineer officers, in 1903, were granted executive rank and titles it was only a question of time until the various clumsy and puzzling compound titles were abolished and a uniform system of rank gradation was introduced. Could anything be more puzzling to the outsider than the fact that a medical officer termed a Surgeon-General was the equal in rank of a Chief Inspector of Machinery, that both were superior in rank to a Paymaster-in-Chief but the equals of a Rear-Admiral? Nor did the titles indicate, except very vaguely, the duties of the officers concerned.

The scheme initiated by Lord Fisher and presented as a Christmas box to a startled Service in 1902, whereby executive officers were to be trained to carry out duties on the bridge or in the engine room as the whim of appointments decided, was bound to be a failure as it did not sufficiently take cognisance of the intense degree of specialisation which rapidly became necessary in both deck and engineer branches.

During the last two years of the War the old titles of the non-executive branches were swept away and executive titles such as Paymaster-Lieutenant were instituted, giving both the professional status and the relative executive rank. This alteration, as far as the engineer officers were concerned, had taken place many years before; but a new breed of engineer officer was gradually coming into his own. This officer did not wear the coloured strip of cloth; he had no compound title but was known as Lieutenant (E) and had rather more executive authority than his predecessors. It was at this time too that the alterations in the uniform already described took place and all officers of whatever branch were placed in the same rate of pay according to their rank. This bore somewhat hardly on some of the senior officers but was ultimately to the advantage of everyone concerned.

The difference between the duties of the executive and the non-executive officers may be widely stated to be that the executive officer exercises control and general supervision over the whole ship, including when necessary the special departments, whilst the non-executive officer exercises local control over his own and no other department. Of course, there is plenty of overlapping in all departments, but as a matter of experience the division of responsibilities and duties indicated works perfectly and, except in isolated and very unusual cases, with perfect efficiency and a minimum of friction. Where the interests of any group of officers clash with those of any other group the dispute is settled by the decision of the senior executive officer. As one of them remarked to me once, 'Somebody has got to say Yes and No, and I am put here to say Yes or No. If I don't agree with you it is because you have failed to make out your case – either it is intrinsically weak or your argument is defective.'

Of course, many points arise which on account of their bearing on general Service conditions the senior executive officer may be unwilling to take the onus of deciding, and in that case the question is referred to the Admiralty through him. Here there is a snag for the unwary reformer of a Nelsonian routine, and on this snag many a promising junior officer has wrecked his career. Destructive criticism unless accompanied by a very real and important suggestion will be followed by extinction of the officer by the Admiralty. As the old Laws of the Navy put it,

> For many are lost and forgotten,
> With nothing to thank for their fate,
> on a half sheet of foolscap
> A fool had the honour to state.

If the constructive suggestion should entail an improvement in the conditions, financial or otherwise, under which the officer is serving he will find himself removed from the appointment before his suggestions are adopted. This is an order to ensure that suggestions are for the benefit of the Service and not for the immediate advantage of the officer concerned. It sounds harsh, but once the principle is conceded it will be found to be perfectly sound and would save much trouble and annoyance if it could be adopted in civilian life.

The head of the ship is the Captain, and he is always known and referred to as the Captain although his naval rank may be that of captain, commander, lieutenant, sub, or gunner, according to the size or importance of the duties of the ship in which he is serving. The Captain is the senior officer of executive rank on board. In the case of our ship the Captain had held that naval rank for several years and was shortly due for automatic promotion to the rank of Admiral. He was tall and slim, and carried himself with a natural dignity of which advantage had been taken when, as a young lieutenant, he had been chosen to carry out the part of the motionless figure standing on the fo'c'sle head of the little *Alberta* as she ploughed her way through the assembled fleets at Spithead with the remains of Queen Victoria on board. The most outstanding memory of that occasion to many of us who were present is our wonder at the iron self-control which supported him in that constrained attitude for nearly two hours. He bore a name which has always been prominent in his country's service in nearly every sphere of activity, but in the Church, perhaps, more than elsewhere. He was an excellent Captain, but one somehow had the feeling that the Navy's gain had meant the loss of a very great bishop. He had a deep regard and constant thought for all who served under him in whatever rank or capacity, and our casualties in action touched him to the quick. On one occasion I read out our list of casualties to him whilst he was still on the bridge after being up all night. His face was grey and unshaven in the cold light of dawn and he seemed to shrink at the mention of each name as it was read out. He had been looking over my shoulder at the list as I read and when it was finished I waited for some remark, but none was made. Turning round I saw his gaze was still fixed on the list and he was muttering the names over to himself. Many of them could have meant nothing to him, but they were his men for whom he felt responsible. All around us wherever we looked we could see signs of losses infinitely greater than anything we had suffered. 'Considering the length of the action it is not a very heavy list,' I said, and even as the words passed my lips I knew it was a futile and banal remark to make. In a voice charged with emotion which all too plainly gave the lie to the words he was using, he replied, 'No; I suppose it's not a very heavy list.... Poor devils.'

The Captain lives in the cuddy in solitary state and, except when he invites one or two of his officers to dine with him, has his meals alone. All heads of departments have direct access to him, receive their leave directly from him, and are consulted by him in all matters concerned with their department. If the Admiralty confer great authority on their Captains they also confer overwhelming responsibility. If an officer lets his captain down in any way he will live to repent it, but their Lordships will hold the captain responsible for the misdeeds of those serving under him.

Apart from those heads of departments who have direct access to the Captain there are many other officers on board, and the medium of communication between them and the Captain is the senior executive officer – the Commander or the 'bloke' as he is affectionately termed on the lower deck. What shall we say about this officer, invariably overworked, and invariably judged and condemned with relentless severity by those above and below him? He must have been of exceptional ability to pass the sifting out process which selected him for promotion from the rank of Lieutenant. Once promoted he will undergo another sifting process before he is promoted to Captain. There is nothing on the face of the waters that is not the duty of the Commander, although I think one of them, a shipmate of mine, was unnecessarily zealous when I found him salving my dirty washing which was swilling round in the bilge water on the floor of my cabin. He is chief housemaid, chief foreman of labourers, chief peacemaker, chief painter, and chief target for criticism. The patience of Job, the tact of a diplomatist, the temper of an archangel, and the vigilance of a lighthouse-keeper would only make a moderately good commander, because on top of all these virtues he must have the power to command men. 'A slack ship is an unhappy ship' is the oldest of sea sayings, so the men must be driven without the yoke being obvious. The happiness and well-being of 1,500 men and the efficiency of the ship as a fighting unit depend on the Commander more than on any other individual officer on board. Have I described a paragon? Perhaps. But I can testify that in over twenty years of sea service I have come across only one bad commander and he would have been a good one if he had been able to take his responsibilities a little less seriously. We had four commanders in the ship during the time I served in her. None lasted long as they were the pick of the Service and were rapidly promoted to Captain. Except one, and he, to his own great content, left his mangled body on the Mole at Zeebrugge.

Chief in authority after the Commander comes the senior lieutenant – the First Lieutenant or 'Jimmy the One.' If the Commander is the foreman of gangers the First Lieutenant is the upper housemaid. He may be a specialist officer such as Gunnery or Torpedo, and on him devolve all the multifarious duties not covered by the Commander's activities. Should he be the Gunnery officer, as he frequently is, his job is one of constant striving from 5.30 in the morning when the hands turn to until rounds are reported correct at 9 p.m. Some idea of the scope of his duties may be learned from the story of the First and Gunnery who was appointed to the Flagship on the China station and who brought his bride to Hong Kong with him. On his arrival on board he reported himself to the Captain and was told the Admiral wished to see him.

'Well, Mr. So-and-so, you have been appointed as First and Gunnery to this ship.'

'Yes, Sir.'

'And I hear you have brought out your wife with you.'

Blushing and somewhat shamefacedly: 'Yes, Sir.'

The Admiral, severely: 'Now tell me, Mr. So-and-so, which do you mean to neglect?'

In the days when spit and polish reigned supreme and the efficiency of a ship was judged solely by the condition of her paintwork and her brightly burnished hammock hooks our First Lieutenant, who was 'salt horse' and so did not have the adventitious aids of Gunnery or Torpedo to help him towards promotion, had also just got married and brought his young wife out to Malta with him. There was no doubt in this case which was the neglected one, but the little lady, herself the daughter of an Admiral and steeped in naval tradition, appreciated the necessity for her husband's aloofness. She did remark, however, that she was glad there were so many other wives attached to the ship, as, from them, she learned something of the ship's and her husband's movements.

This separation of naval husbands and wives is not such a serious question nowadays as it was some thirty years ago. At a dinner party at Sheerness, a sweet young thing, who had just become engaged to one of our officers, was seated on the left of the Commander-in-Chief at the Nore, an exceptionally bluff and hearty seaman of the old school. He was very antagonistic to the marriage of junior officers, and having been informed by a casual remark of the engagement he proceeded to ingratiate himself by decrying marriage as the ruin of a naval officer's career – 'A sailor's wife a sailor's ship should be' sort of thing. He went on in this strain for some time, to the evident distress of the lady, but when he dilated also on the disadvantages of naval marriage from the wife's point of view she began to take command of the situation and argued. The Admiral, unused to opposition, finally brought out his trump card.

'I was foolish enough to get married as a young officer, was sent to sea a couple of months afterwards, and didn't see my wife again for ten years.'

'And was that why you wrote "Hurrah for the life of a sailor," Sir William?'

The inference concealed in the lady's remark nearly gave the old gentleman a fit, and he hastily dropped the subject of marriage amongst naval officers.

After 'Jimmy the One' comes the group of Lieutenant-Commanders or Lieutenants who may be specialists such as Navigators, Gunnery etc., or just plain 'salt horse' as the watch-keeping lieutenant is called who has no specialist qualification. These officers were also subject to constant change on board our ship as they were selected for promotion to Commander or were appointed to other ships. One of our watchkeepers had retired from the Service a few years before and started an insurance agency on shore which was doing well until the stress of war brought him back to the Service. In an effort at keeping up his business he used to tell us lurid stories of the risks we were running, and the advisability of ensuring a cash result from our misfortunes. He had little success as few amongst us were altruistic enough to wish to soften the blow to our relations by the *quid pro quo*. It was only when one of our junior officers pointed out to him that he was running the very risks he considered so terrible for us that he gave it up. In his professional zeal he had forgotten that these arguments applied to him just as much as to us.

Of course, during the War we carried temporary officers as well and they belonged either to the Royal Naval Reserve or the Royal Naval Volunteer Reserve. From the pattern of stripes on their sleeves they were nicknamed the Wavy Navy. Our R.N.R. lieutenant was a fine example of that patriotic body culled from the flower of our Merchant Service. He was a Scotsman and in times of peace the chief officer of a large liner. Naturally he was much older than the average lieutenant but by the Service regulations he was junior in rank to similar officers on the active list. It is a difficult position for a man accustomed to almost unlimited authority in his own sphere of life to hold himself subordinate in another sphere which has so many points of resemblance to his own. It must be remembered that the fighting efficiency of the ship depends very largely on the good feeling and perfect co-operation of the men who man her. There are so many situations which printed regulations cannot cover, however strictly worded, even though obeyed to the letter – and it is the letter that kills the spirit at sea as elsewhere – that only a perfect harmony of fellowship can hold the balance evenly between the clashing interests concerned. It was here that our Scotsman shone, and he slipped into his niche in the ship's economy like an otter taking to the water.

It has been my lot to travel frequently on board merchant vessels and I have always been struck by the high standard of discipline amongst their crews. True, the standard of discipline on board a man-of-war is high, but in the last resort its enforcement is backed up by a penal code, a special branch of ship's police, cells and if necessary detention quarters as the naval prisons are euphemistically termed. There is no such parallel on board a merchant ship. The most the master can do to a delinquent is to fine him a couple of day's pay and portentously enter his name in the ship's log duly countersigned by the mate. In very extreme cases the offender may be put in irons and prosecuted before the civil authority on the ship's arrival in port. Few ship masters will face the latter procedure as it involves detention of the ship and demurrage charges. The final result of any action taken is that it may or may not affect the man's character on discharge, but that has no real terror for a good seaman as it will not prevent him getting a job as soon as he is ready for one. Yet with so slight a hold as that indicated the discipline on board a British merchant ship is of so high a standard that any seasoned sea traveller who knows anything about a ship beyond the shortest route to the cocktail bar will always travel British rather than foreign – just in case. I can quote plenty of instances to support this argument, but one will suffice. Some years ago on a dark and stormy night a foreign ship carrying a large number of passengers fell across the ram of a British man-of-war lying in Gibraltar Bay and was sunk. Every effort at rescue was made, but the casualties were out of all proportion high, and it was not until the dead were examined that the cause was found. Many of them had been stabbed in the back, evidently by people behind, whilst struggling up companion ways. The wounds all corresponded to injuries inflicted by sheath knives such as were commonly carried by seamen of the day.

This high degree of British discipline will almost certainly be denied by the very men who are responsible for its inculcation, and a long winded statement in which the adjectives are numerous and powerful whilst the nouns are few and feeble will guarantee its absence from the particular ship under discussion. Suggest, as I have often done, to the heated detractor of his countrymen that he would probably be better off with a crew of any other specified or unspecified nationality and the argument will at once fade out with 'Well you see, I don't know – in an emergency.'

The basis of all discipline in both merchant and fighting ships is character, and the point I am trying to bring out is that the merchant service officer has to depend almost entirely on character for his results, and that he gets them.

So it will not surprise anyone to learn that 'Jock' was just as popular on the lower deck as he was in the wardroom and that the bugle for the captain's defaulters was rarely a signal to be feared by any of the men under his charge. He served his country well at the cost of his career in his own company, but Trinity House must be a sweeter place for his presence.

Our R.N.V.R. officers were a mixed bag. The Volunteer Reserve had been a very small branch of the auxiliary Naval Service, but when officers for numberless minor duties had to be entered at all costs, these temporary officers were usually granted commissions in the Volunteer Reserve. We had three such lieutenants on board. Two of them had been civilian schoolmasters at the Royal Naval College but when Dartmouth was closed down at the beginning of the War and all the cadets were drafted to ships they were given commissions and sent to our ship. It was sheer waste of manpower as both men were of brilliant attainments, and a very moderate degree of intelligence would have been sufficient to cope with the duties delegated to them. In time the mistake was rectified and they were sent to another sphere of activity, but we always remembered their cheerfulness and good temper when, in an uncongenial atmosphere, they toiled diligently at the brain-benumbing task of decoding. The third member of this group was a character and I should say without hesitation the most popular officer on board. He was known as Mike and, needless to say, the name had nothing to do with baptismal records.

Mike was the younger brother of a well-known and popular naval officer, and for a year or two before the outbreak of war he had been trying to delude himself into the belief that he was a heaven-born civil engineer. He had an office in town which had somehow escaped the notice of possible clients, so that when the world went mad on August 4th, 1914, he had no compunction about locking it up in order that he might wend his way to the nearest recruiting office. There he was asked which Service he wished to join, and with memories of an exceedingly good looking brother in a very attractive uniform he chose the Navy and was handed over to a recruiting Chief Petty Officer. Mike was a sizeable lad and the recruiter felt he had drawn a prize.

'Now, my lad, what was your civilian profession?'

Mike explained that he had been trained as a civil engineer. The C.P.O. listened to the engineer but considered the civil redundant.

'Engineer, was yer? Then yer ought to join up as a stoker.'

Mike demurred. He didn't know much about the lower deck occupations but he had a shrewd suspicion that stoking was not likely to prove a happy high road towards fame and a commission, the urgent constraint towards both of which had induced him to enlist.

'Now, young feller me lad! You listen to me wot knows. I'm telling yer. Ye join as a stoker, two bob a day an' everything found. You sees the world, ye cocks a chest, and all yer has to do is to turn on a tap to let the oil fuel run into the furnaces. And yer gets to sea straight away before this war is over. All the other blinking perishers won't 'ave 'alf finished their training when you'll be drawing yer batter money.'

The last consideration settled the question of his war employment for Mike. He must get to sea before the war was over, and so he became a stoker. Needless to say, in view of the recruiter's activities, that the navy was short of stokers at the time.

After a fortnight's intensive training at a depot, where he learned that stoking had little to do with the turning on of taps but a great deal to do with the attitude best adapted for manipulating a heavy shovelful of coal, and the correct method of clearing a sluggish fire with a devilishly awkward weapon called a 'slice', Mike was kitted up and, complete with bag and hammock, was drafted to a light cruiser which was innocent of taps and oil fuel.

He never voluntarily talked much about his experiences as a stoker, but we used to question him about his life on the lower deck. Curiously enough although most of us had lived within elbow distance of the mess decks for the best part of our lives none of us had any idea what it was really like, and how it would affect a gently nurtured man. He rarely said much against it, but one evening he let himself go when we had been discussing some of the signs of Communism which the temporary ratings had introduced into the Fleet. I had said that I should like to live amongst them as one of themselves so that one could learn what was wrong and take steps to remedy any real grievances. His reply was very much to the point.

'You'd loathe it.'

'Would I? Is it so bad as all that?'

'Yes. You couldn't stand the constant use of bad language, the complete lack of privacy at all times, the way your food is slung at you, and your messmates' table manners.'

'The bad language?' This was a new idea to me. Dr. Johnson's 'term of endearment among sailors' had always been looked upon as an archaic joke not in the best of taste.

'Yes. You've always been in the position of an officer. You don't really know anything about life on the mess deck. At first when I joined I thought I could swear and curse with the best, but the filthy adjectives with which the most casual remark was plastered nearly made me sick. Gradually I got accustomed to it and didn't mind so much. That is the position of the men themselves. They have lost their sense of the meaning of the words they use, and the foulest epithet means nothing to them at all, so little that an extra foulness is only a joke to be remembered and improved upon if possible.'

'But if words have become sounds with no special meaning attached to them need they affect one as foul language?'

Mike eyed me suspiciously. 'I don't like your argument and it wouldn't hold water for five minutes if you had to sit on a wooden stool at a wooden mess-table along with twenty foul-mouthed jokers from 7.30 until 9.30 every night of your life. A dirty joke should be funny in spite of the dirt, but when the joke lies in the dirt it gives me the dry heaves.'

'What about the want of privacy?'

'You never get away from your fellow men. You bathe starko amongst a crowd who will pass the most dreadful remarks about your physical development which is open for all to see; you undress to the buff leaning against another sweaty body which means to turn in in the flannels it has been wearing all day; you sleep in a hammock jammed so closely amongst other hammocks that you can feel every movement and hear every breath and snort of the men on either side of you; you write your letters with somebody leaning over your shoulder and reading as if it were the most natural thing in the world; and if the post doesn't bring you a letter from a girl a good-natured messmate will offer, you a dekko at his – "a good spicy one, mate." And he will expect you to read it and give your opinion of the writer.'

'Sounds pretty awful,' I said, 'and would take a lot of getting used to. But you can't really complain about the grub. Dash it all, it's part of my job to see that it is all right and I've never seen anything one could reasonably complain to the Paymaster about.'

Mike grinned. 'I've never complained about the grub. I distinctly said I couldn't stand the way it was slung at you. The way it is dished up and served would only be tolerated by an amateur yachtsman.' He got up and fled as I aimed a blow at him with the grummet I was making. All the mess knew about my yachting proclivities.

Mike's release from the lower deck came about in an unusual fashion. Part of the Nelson routine which, along with the Nelson spirit but in a much greater ratio, has been passed on to his successors is the manner of rousing the weary lower deck sleeper to the delights of a new day. The bugle goes at 5.30 a.m. and thereafter the messdecks are bombarded with shouts of 'Show a leg there! Show a leg! Show a leg or a purser's stocking!' alternating with 'Lash up and stow! Lash up and stow!' Whilst this uproar assaults the ears the ship's police go round the hammocks and if anyone is unduly slow in leaving his frowsty nest he is either pulled out or ejected by the petty officer stooping under the sagging hammock, putting his shoulder under the most prominent part of the sluggard's anatomy, and then standing up. The immediate result is to capsize the man ('Purser's stockings' on women are unknown nowadays) out of the hammock on to the deck after making violent contact with knobbly things such as messtables and stools during the transit. On one particular morning Mike was not wakened either by the bugle or the din of the piping and he was rudely roused by finding himself a bruised heap on the mess deck. Furiously angry, he struck out wildly at the ship's corporal who was standing grinning at him, caught him under the chin and laid him out. Revenge was sweet, but the sweetness was woefully short lived. He was immediately seized by two other ship's corporals, fairly roughly handled, forced to dress and then dragged to the quarter-deck before the officer of the watch where he was charged with the very serious offence of striking his superior officer whilst in the execution of his duty.

It is necessary to make some remarks about the heinousness of this offence, as it is no unusual thing to hear violent criticism of the Service attitude towards it and the apparently vindictive punishment meted out. Let it be understood, therefore, that the brunt of the offence is not in striking but in the fact that the striker is assaulting someone who cannot strike back and whose efforts at defending himself, except in case of dire necessity, will be looked upon with suspicion as probably justifying the assault – another serious offence. Should the senior strike the junior it will in all probability mean the end of the senior's career in the service; for a certainty if the senior is a commissioned officer.

The officer of the watch recognised that Mike's case was beyond his jurisdiction, so the stoker was placed under the sentry's charge whilst the twenty-four hours passed which the Regulations insist upon as the interval between the commission of an offence and its investigation. At 'Captain's defaulters' he was remanded for further investigation, as his offence was one which in the piping times of peace would have been dealt with by Court Martial empowered to award a sentence of anything up to two years' imprisonment in Naval Detention Quarters. Naval Courts Martial are characterised by 'devilish little law but a hell of a lot of justice.' At least that is how they were described by a well-known solicitor who, on account of his vast experience and knowledge of the vagaries of naval law, was the favourite 'prisoner's friend' at the courts held in one of our ports. If he had been briefed to appear the prisoner felt that no matter what the result everything possible had been done for him, which comforted in much the same curious way as the calling in of a specialist does the sorrowing heirs of a dying testator. Without his help the offender 'never had no chance' and a life-long grievance. Needless to say his activities were always viewed with a certain amount of trepidation by all the naval officers who were liable to serve on a court as naval law is only a very small and infrequent issue in the hotch-potch duties of an executive officer, and he knows just enough law to teach him a wholesome respect for the expert. Though as long as we have Civil Courts of Appeal no naval officer need feel ashamed of the Court Martial returns, on their legal aspect at any rate.

Just before the War the solicitor in question had been employed to act as 'prisoner's friend' in a rather unusual case. On board one of the destroyers in reserve, the Commanding Officer and the Chief Engineer were both warrant officers and were on very bad terms with one another. There had been constant quarrelling and it was well known that each had stated on more than one occasion that he was out for the other's blood – 'wanted his guts for a necktie' in the vulgar language of the low sailor man. One morning, whilst manoeuvring his ship away from the trot at which she was lying, the gunner on the bridge telegraphed full speed astern on the starboard engine as the ship was getting too near to her next ahead and he wanted to slew her out of line. The reply to this from the engine room was full speed ahead, and with a crash the next ahead got it in the stern whilst the crumpled bows of the destroyer herself effectually negatived any sea work for a long time to come.

There was the usual preliminary work in the way of enquiries, reports and circumstantial letters, and finally the engineer officer was ordered to be tried by Court Martial for disobedience of orders. He briefed our solicitor and awaited the result with some hope and a good deal of fear. There was not the faintest doubt that he was at fault, and a sudden termination of his Service career seemed inevitable.

The court was presided over by a Captain, and the evidence given by the prosecutor was beyond dispute. The solicitor sat quite still whilst all the points for the prosecution were being made, and to the dismay of the prisoner, and the obvious discomfort of the members of the Court, declined to cross-examine any of the witnesses or to take any part in the proceedings beyond that of a slightly bored spectator. Finally the prosecuting officer said that the case for the prosecution was completed and the presiding officer ordered the case for the defence to be opened.

The solicitor was galvanised into life at last and he addressed the President.

'Am I to understand that the case for the prosecution is closed, Sir?'

'Yes, certainly. You have just heard me say so.'

'And I am to understand that in no circumstances can the case for the prosecution be reopened?'

'No. No. I tell you, we will proceed at once with the defence.'

'Then since the case for the prosecution is closed I submit to the Court, Sir, that my friend has no case to answer!'

The Court gasped; the Prosecutor felt his heart passing rapidly through his stomach and seeking swift and permanent contact with his boots; the President gaped at the solicitor like a child who has been told there is no birthday present for him.

'I don't grasp your point, Mr. Solicitor.'

'I submit to the Court that my client has no case, in law, to answer.'

The President looked more puzzled than ever and then he gave the order 'Clear the Court.'

The Court was cleared. Prisoner, witnesses, spectators, and solicitor were bundled out whilst the members pooled their startled wits in an effort at finding out what the confident assurance of the lawyer meant. They knew him too well to doubt that he was completely justified in his contention. But on what grounds? Surely there had never been a clearer case! What had this limb of Satan got up his sleeve this time? They talked and argued and gave it up. The Court was re-assembled.

The President looked at the lawyer and liked his confident attitude less and less. There would be a pretty kettle of fish for him to fry if his conduct of the Court had been at fault.

'I understand you to claim that your friend has, in law, no case to answer?'

'That is my opinion and I have every reason to believe it is correct.'

'Would you kindly explain to the Court your grounds for that opinion?'

'Certainly. The prosecution has omitted to prove that my friend was in the engine room at the time of the alleged occurrence.'

It was quite true and a hasty glance at the typewritten report of the proceedings only confirmed the lawyer's argument. The case was busted and once again law had won in its long and deadly strife with justice. But it was long before the legal department of the Admiralty allowed possible members of Courts to forget this incident. In fact, I believe that if it hadn't been for a little trouble between 1914 and 1918 they would still be worrying at it.

I had an amusing episode once when I was mixed up with the legal department and a compensation case which the Admiralty were disputing. It was a case of a workman suffering from paralysis which was in no way due to his occupation although he claimed that it was. I have heard liars classed as liars, damned liars and expert witnesses, and it was as a member of the third class that I had to endure a long and tedious journey from Scapa Flow to give evidence in the case. Whilst seated in the solicitor's office and going over my evidence, which was plentifully backed up by important authorities, a higher official came in and abruptly announced that the case would not be called after all. A little bit nettled, as I was entirely responsible for the case being fought, I asked why.

'Because we are going to settle the case out of Court.'

'Have the opposite side seen sense at last and dropped it?'

'No. We are going to admit liability and pay compensation on the agreed scale.'

I was very angry that my beautifully worked up case should be treated in this fashion.

'But I assure you beyond a shadow of a doubt that I can produce authorities –'

The official cut me short. 'You can produce anything you like. The other side are going to produce the patient in court lying on a stretcher with a doctor and a nurse in attendance. No British jury is going to stand out against that kind of appeal! It's a lot cheaper to settle out of court.'

But we left Mike in the sentry's charge, waiting for the Captain's decision how he was to be dealt with. That officer was worried quite a lot as he knew there were some unusual elements in the case. Mike had admitted his offence at once, said he was half-asleep when he committed it, he had not recognised the ship's Corporal and merely thought it was time to stop the series of practical jokes to which he had been subjected ever since he had joined up. He apologised and expressed regret. His explanation and apology would have been accepted at once and he would have been discharged with a caution had it not been for two considerations which weighed heavily on the Captain's mind. The first was that it was evident to the Captain, as well as to his messmates who used to chip him about it, that Mike belonged to a much higher social body than was usual on the lower deck and any leniency might be interpreted as undue consideration on account of that social standing. The other reason was that punishment is held on board ship to be much more valuable as a deterrent than as vengeance or cure for crime. If Mike's excuse passed muster it would be difficult on a future occasion to reject a similar plea, and any ruffian might swot an unpopular petty officer and expect to get away with it by saying it was all a mistake. So the puzzled Captain ordered Mike back again to the sentry's charge while he considered the case anew.

In the meantime, unknown to Mike and the Captain, the Fates were taking a hand in the game and rapidly moving to extricate both from the dilemma in which they were placed.

The naval officer brother had been horrified when he heard that Mike had joined up and was actually serving as a stoker, and had started pulling strings. Being a man of considerable influence professionally, as well as socially, he could pull good and hearty, and his representations about his brother were listened to. The result was that before Mike was due to appear before the Captain and receive the sentence of ten days cells which was the minimum punishment the Captain felt he could inflict, that officer was astonished to receive a communication from the Admiralty informing him that Stoker Second Class Mike had been granted a commission as Lieutenant R.N.V.R. and that he was to be discharged to the Depot forthwith. There still remained the tangle of the assault to be cleared up, but a glance at the order showed that the date of the Commission was prior to the date of the assault, so the charge of striking his superior officer must fall to the ground, though the equally grave offence of striking a subordinate still held good. The Captain, tickled to tears to learn that his insubordinate stoker was the brother of one of his best friends, told Mike to square matters with the ship's Corporal as best he could. The latter on having the affair explained to him was highly amused, accepted Mike's apology as well as the coloured plaster tendered, and all was well. An apology is always a serious matter in the Service and is a difficult thing to get. It is never looked upon lightly either by the giver or receiver, and has been defined as the only redress for injury an officer can give or receive, with honour, from another. It is a highly formal affair and bears no relationship to the casual 'Sorry' of civilian life.

His chrysalis stage as a stoker being finished Mike went to Barracks, shed his grubby square rig covering and emerged as a full-blown butterfly lieutenant. As a stoker he might have been a success because he possessed to the full the special qualifications necessary for that grimy and arduous occupation; but he was a first class lieutenant and an ideal messmate.

Amongst our other officers we carried a Captain and subaltern of Marines. The old sea soldier, recruited originally to protect the naval officer from the piratical attentions of his pressed crew, still holds his place of honour on board his Majesty's ships and vessels by right of long service and proved value. Still, as in Nelson's time, the marines' mess is situated on the lower deck between the seamen's and the officers' quarters. Kipling's eulogy of the 'soldier and sailor too' still holds good as we all know it will, as long as the meddlesome heads will allow them to remain as one of the fighting units of the fleet. Our Captain of Marines was an exceptional man even amongst that fine body. He was one of the best looking men I have ever seen; he had the much envied letters P.S.C. after his name on the Navy List, indicating that he had successfully surmounted the brain-storming training of the Staff College, and he had a temper that nothing in this world could ruffle. In a navy whose members depend chiefly on their uniform for the success of their assaults on the feminine heart, the excessive good looks of our Marine were at first looked upon as indicating the vacuous brains popularly associated with such an appearance. Never was a greater mistake. He could give the best of us ten yards in a hundred in a mental sprint and beat us hands down. To those of us less generously endowed his share of good things seemed to be hardly quite fair.

One of the oldest duties of the Marines, dating from the days when they were literally the protectors of the officers, was that of providing personal servants. Not altogether to the officers' advantage, a movement had been set on foot before the War to abolish the Marine servant altogether, and boy domestics specially enrolled for that purpose were being detailed to ships after a period of training in the depots. The change had been necessitated by the fact that in many of the smaller ships no Marines were carried and consequently the officers' servants had to be supplied by volunteers from the lower deck ratings and this had proved highly unsatisfactory. The supply of these domestics was not yet equal to the demand when our ship commissioned, so that we were lucky enough to have Marine servants to attend to our simple needs.

The servant is a volunteer, he receives extra pay at the rate of £1 to £1 10s. a month from his master, he is excused certain of his duties as a Marine such as sentry work, and there are various dietetic perquisites from the officers' galley. You may get an experienced servant or you may not. The first I ever had was entirely new to the game but he had been well coached by the Corporal of Marine servants so that he was reasonably efficient. But he had one serious fault. My cabin was very small and when he came in about 6.30 a.m. to brush my clothes and get my bath ready there was no convenient place for him to get to work. So he used to spread the garments on my bunk on top of my recumbent and somnolent form and get going with a vigour which would have delighted the heart of any naval tailor. Life on board a battleship will teach one to sleep under the most adverse conditions and I was pretty well hardened, but this was too much. If I protested vigorously and told him to take the adjectival things out of my cabin and spread them on a midshipman's chest in the flat outside, he would do so; but the very next morning the same thing would happen again. Finally I was forced to accept the solution of the difficulty suggested by the Captain of the Marines. I got up as soon as he came in and shaved to the accompaniment of swish, swish from the brush and hiss, hiss, hiss through the closed teeth of the servant. Of course he had been a farmer's boy.

My Marine servant during the War was of a different type altogether. His real and his Service ages were separated by an indefinite but considerable number of years, and at forty-nine he looked over sixty. He had completed his twenty-one years in the Service some time before the outbreak of the War and had retired to the suburbs of Malvern, where he worked as a barber in a little room behind his shop whilst his better half dispensed newspapers, sweets, tobacco, and gossip in front. He was very elderly, grey, conscientiously slow and, being a barber, his back hair was constantly in need of trimming. Usually he was the ordinary Marine servant, faithful, diligent, and a trifle heavy handed, and his conversation was strictly limited to 'Yes, Sir', and 'No, Sir'. But for an hour once a fortnight and at the rate of 1s. a time he became my barber, and a totally different character emerged. I would receive a message from another servant that the barber was ready for me in my cabin, and on arriving there I would find the floor had been cleared of its carpet, a chair had been planted in the middle of it, and with last week's sheet from my bed draped over his arm the barber was completely in command of the situation. He would say 'Good morning' or 'Good afternoon' – words that are usually anathema in any well-conducted ship – remark that the weather had been very unsatisfactory of late, and, as he draped the sheet over my shoulders and tucked it in at the back of my neck, ask me how I liked it. The routine reply of short back and sides was always acknowledged with an expression of gratitude, and thereafter to the clip, clip of the scissors there was the usual tonsorial flow of language on every subject under the sun. He avoided the subject of the War. It had interfered with his business and he dared not let himself go. My contribution to the conversation was confined by tacit agreement to 'yes' and 'no' in all the modulations the English language permits. These monologues were intensely interesting as they kept me in touch with the spirit of the lower deck and the reactions of a simple loyal spirit to the stress of the War. Having expressed, quite untruthfully, my satisfaction with the result of his labours ('You've had one of these grass cutters at you again, Sir' as my favourite barber in town remarked once when I was on leave) the barber proceeded to sweep up the mess and disappeared for another fortnight.

It is difficult to believe that an officer of the calibre of our Captain of Marines could serve for over two years in the finest fighting ship afloat, be present at all the actions in the North Sea which could be described as of major importance, and finally leave the ship at his own urgent request for a staff appointment at the front without having been awarded a single ribbon to record the Admiralty appreciation of his worth. The fact was that his job gave little scope for a display of his ability, but when I saw him again at the end of the War it was easy to see that he had been appreciated by the army. His breast simply sprouted medals and decorations.

The question of decorations must be a subject of constant ill feeling amongst those who set great store by them. The only safe and satisfactory solution of the subject is no decorations at all, but I'm afraid that is a counsel of perfection. A cynical admiral once remarked: 'When you present a decoration you only please one individual and you annoy a thousand.' At the beginning of the War the head of the Medical Department set his face strongly against the presentation of decorations to any of his officers, on the grounds that no matter what their merits they had only carried out their duty. So I was not surprised nor disappointed when the Admiral told me that he had sent my name up three times for a decoration and that it had been blocked by my own department. It didn't matter as we were all very much in the same boat. A year later when I was in Wei hai Wei what was my astonishment to read in an Admiralty Monthly Order that decorations had been granted to two medical officers of the Battle Cruiser fleet for their services at Jutland. I began to feel annoyed and wrote to the Admiralty that, though officially recommended, I had never received one and that these two officers who had been granted them had not only never been recommended but had not been present at the Battle of Jutland in any capacity. I added somewhat bitterly that it was little to the credit of the Medical Department that they didn't even know which of their officers were present in action. I received no acknowledgement of my letter, but a later monthly order cancelled the decorations granted to these two officers and gave me one – of a grade lower than those given to the absentees.

Years ago when I was serving in the Mediterranean we had an admiral who joined the Fleet with a solitary decoration on his capacious chest. In an effort at remedying this unseemly state of affairs he arranged to be present with his flagship and some portion of his Fleet at every function of any importance along the shores of the Mediterranean. Soon there was to be seen above his heart the multi-coloured evidence of the attainment of his heart's desire. Towards the end of his appointment he had laid every maritime country under contribution with the exception of Turkey, and of course the difficulty about Turkey was that the Dardanelles were closed to the passage of men-of-war. Just before his return to England he got his chance. The Fleet was lying at Mudros and he wangled an invitation for himself and his family to visit Constantinople on board the Admiral's yacht, which, not being armed, was entitled to pass through the Straits. The visit was duly paid and the Sultan was much impressed by the Admiral but charmed to distraction by the Admiral's beautiful daughters, and small blame to him. In due course the Sultan announced his appreciation of the visit by conferring upon the Admiral the order of the Lia Kat and upon the daughters the Order of Chastity – of the Second Class. Poor girls! Luckily father's reign was nearly over.

One of our chaplains was a temporary officer who had joined up immediately after war had been declared. He was a good-looking young bachelor with a very pleasant voice, and his departure from the curacy of a large and fashionable West End church had been the signal for much drooping of feminine spirits, under whose adulation a very fine character was rapidly becoming enervated. His arrival in a wardroom of thirty-three officers, many of whom did not belong to his denomination and not one of whom was prepared to accept him as a chaplain until they were satisfied with him as a man amongst men, must have been an exceedingly trying experience after his rose-scented progress through Mayfair. Except when employed in the duties of his office he received exactly the same consideration from his messmates as would have been accorded to any other officer of his age. Wisely, the naval regulations do not provide a relative rank for the chaplain, so that his position in the mess depends entirely on his character; and just at first we were not inclined to admire that character. There was a suspicion that the aristocratic surroundings of his curacy were reflecting glory on the incumbent and the names of society leaders were just a little too frequently on his lips. The complete indifference with which his eulogies were listened to caused a certain amount of shock to his ideas of what was just and proper, and the last appearance of this phase was on the day when he was trying to impress one of our lieutenants with the name of one of his most distinguished admirers.

'Terrible old woman,' was the lieutenant's reply. 'I wonder you can stand her.'

'But,' gasped the horrified chaplain, 'she's the Countess of Broadacres!'

'Oh, yes, I know,' said the lieutenant; 'she's my aunt.'

The rest of us who were listening to this conversation knew about the relationship although the chaplain did not. Later one of us asked the lieutenant whether the old lady was so terrible as he made out. 'She's a dear really. But she loves a good story and if that chaplain doesn't behave himself she is going to get one.'

Officers and men alike are subject to compulsory church and for purposes of attendance at the religious services are divided into three groups – Church of England, Roman Catholics and Tubthumpers. The attitude of philosophic doubt is not recognised as it would upset the funeral routine if nobody knew under which, if any, halo the deceased should be buried. The Church of England service is held on the mess deck in bad weather and under the awning on the quarter-deck in fine, after divisions on Sunday morning. Small evening services are accommodated in one of the gun casemates and are not compulsory like the morning one. If you belong to the Church of England only sickness or duty are accepted as excuses for non-attendance. A Roman Catholic priest is carried on board one of the ships where there is a largish fleet and he holds services as requisite on board one ship, to which his flock is sent in boats from the other ships. The Tubthumpers are not usually in large enough numbers to justify the carrying of a special chaplain, but on Sundays in port a church party is fallen in and, under the orders of an officer of their own sect, they are sent ashore to seek spiritual comfort and refreshment in one of the civilian establishments.

On board one ship the Commander was very keen on all officers attending church and he was much annoyed to find that a recently joined officer, without obvious reason, had absented himself from church on two successive Sundays. He gave him a talking to and the officer, who had agnostic leanings, explained that he could not attend church as he had objections to the use of a liturgy.

'But damn it all, man! The lower deck have got to attend church. Why the devil should you be let off and them not?'

'Well, you see, I am Church of Scotland.' The only argument he could bring forward in substantiation of that claim was his patronymic, which had a northern ring.

The Commander looked doubtful. 'Yes, I see. A Presbyterian.'

Now there are many Presbyterian churches scattered throughout the coastal towns of England but there are few if any Church of Scotland ones.

'No, no. Church of Scotland.'

'What the devil's the difference?' growled the Commander.

'Well, Sir, it's a matter of conscience.'

'Conscience! roared the Commander. 'Conscience!' and then he gave it up. Any language he knew fitted to deal with this claim for conscience struck him as being ludicrously unsuitable to the subject under discussion.

So the conscientious one reaped the benefit of his conscience and, for several Sunday mornings while the rest of his messmates were at church, he enjoyed the Sabbath calm in the seclusion of the wardroom, tucked away in the most comfortable easy chair and with the pick of the Sunday papers at his elbow. Apparently the Commander had forgotten all about the matter.

Some weeks afterwards the Fleet anchored in a large harbour on the coast of Scotland, and as the Fleet was large, the head of the harbour shallow, and the ship the tail of the line she anchored about three miles from the landing place, which was inside a broken down tidal harbour. The first Sunday morning in their new billet broke grey and cold, with a strong southwest wind sweeping across the foam-flecked harbour and bringing squalls of sleet and rain with it at frequent intervals. The Commander had retired to his cabin after breakfast and from there sent a message to the conscience-stricken one that he was to come at once and see him before divisions. The order was duly obeyed.

'Mr. Conscience! You are to take charge of the Presbyterian Church party and conduct them to the Scotch Church on shore. Service begins at 12 o'clock so you will fall in with the church party at 11.15 and the picket-boat will tow you ashore in the cutter. You will sail the boat back, as you have a nice fair wind. The picket-boat is not to enter the harbour, as the tide is falling. I've warned the minister you are coming, but there aren't enough of you to justify a special service so you are attending the ordinary service.'

The only answer a naval officer is entitled to make on receiving an order is 'Aye, aye, Sir,' and of course it was duly forthcoming. But there were many thoughts that lay too deeply for words.

At 11.15 a.m. the wretched church-goers were dragged away from the cosy warmth of the messdecks where the others were just beginning to settle down after the short and comfortable ship's church, embarked on board the cutter, and the tow astern of the picket-boat in the teeth of half a gale of wind and rain began. The officer had tried to gain the shelter of the picket-boat's cabin but the Commander negatived this and gave orders to the midshipman in charge of the boat to proceed with all possible dispatch, drop the cutter half a mile from the inner harbour, and return to the ship at once as the boat was required for urgent duties.

For nearly 3 miles of rough sea the picket-boat midshipman carried out his orders with a fidelity which argued well for his future in the Service. The miserable occupants of the cutter were towed at 14 knots right into the teeth of it, and as the only shelter provided was their oilskins they were soon drenched to the skin and half frozen with cold. With blue faces and chattering teeth they stuck it out as well as they could, and when finally cast off the scratch crew were so numb that they could hardly get the boat into the landing place, to the intense amusement of some fishermen who had come down to the jetty to greet and criticise their arrival. The crew had been warmed up a little by their rowing, but the officer was compelled to endure the privilege of his rank and do nothing.

The party was fallen in on the quayhead and marched to the dour little church which purveyed their particular brand of soul saving. Thanks to the weather they were a bit late and they entered the church just as the beadle was slamming the door of the pulpit after the minister's entrance. The divine gazed sternly at them until the elders had marshalled them into such seats as were vacant and then fell on his knees, with his hands clasped over his head, facing the cushion on which the enormous bible rested and apparently prayed that the wrath to come might strike his visitors quick and sure.

But for a Scots minister, he did not take unfair advantage of his temporary adherents. It is true he lengthened his usual discourse from an hour to an hour and a half and from a usual Thirdly to a Fifthly, but he did cut out the Gaelic address – and thereby raised some doubts in the minds of his flock as to whether he might not be pandering to the Scarlet Woman – so that by 3.15 his dazed and jaded listeners were able to get back to their boat. There they found that the two boat-keepers had succumbed to the temptations of a nearby shebeen, and then, full of some of the worst that masquerades under the name of Scotch, they had racketed round the town raising Cain and had finally disappeared. After a fruitless search of half an hour the officer gave them up and sailed back to his ship minus two of his crew. To add insult to injury the Commander did not like the way he brought his boat alongside under canvas and sent them away to do it again.

It was the final straw. They had been thoroughly soaked and frozen, they had missed their Sunday dinner, which is usually an extra good one, they had lost two of their crew and would have to explain things at 'defaulters' next day. On the other hand they had listened to an inspiring address on the

Athanasian Creed ... The upshot of the affair can be gathered from a remark Mr. Conscience was heard to make over a gin and bitters later in the evening.

'Proselytizing, I call it, that sort of treatment!'

Our chaplain had the knack of winning the confidence of the lower deck, and his efforts were rewarded when we were in action. Nominally he belonged to the first aid party but, like the rest of us, he found the period of waiting doing nothing while the battle was raging overhead frightfully trying, and he found ease and comfort for his own strained nerves by wandering round the decks and bringing his kindly human interest to bear upon others similarly situated. When work of a grim and revolting nature arrived he was ready for it, despite a natural shrinking from such unaccustomed sights. As soon as his services could be spared he was ready to tender such spiritual consolation as the general conditions and the state of the patients admitted. When he left the ship for another appointment the fashionable curate had gone for ever and he was simply and affectionately accepted everywhere as 'our padre.'

Our Engineer Commander controlled the work lives of 700 men and the mighty output of 120,000 horsepower which, delivered to our four gigantic propellers, could drive the mass of 33,000 tons at over 32 knots. If figures so great can convey anything, they will give some idea of his responsibilities and the knowledge necessary to use our powers to the best possible advantage. He had 'built the ship,' that is to say he had been appointed to her long before she was completed, and had a complete mastery of every bit of machinery in her. How he did it one was never able to guess because to all appearances he took more interest in his beautifully kept finger nails and his immaculate uniform than in anything else on board. But I have been sitting talking to him in his cabin where I could hear nothing but the subdued hum of distant machinery and seen him suddenly jump to his telephone because his subconscious mind had recognised a faint alteration in the rhythm which spelt danger. The only alteration he ever made in his uniform when he went down into his engine room was to draw on a pair of huge gauntlet gloves, and even they were spotless on his return. He was amazing and unbelievable because he meant so much to the ship, and yet without any suggestion of posing he conveyed the impression that he was superfluous and unnecessary, except as a figurehead for his department. But if you had any difficulties which could in any way be considered the business of his department they vanished with his nod and queer little half smile which was the most of assent he ever allowed himself.

On one occasion whilst we were at sea I was wakened about 3 a.m. by the officer of the watch stumbling in agony into my cabin. He had been brought down from the bridge by a quartermaster because he had been suddenly seized with a bolt of excruciating pain. A minute's examination was enough to make my diagnosis. Perforated gastric ulcer. Operation was urgently necessary. If performed within twelve hours he would surely recover, within twenty-four hours he would probably recover. Delay beyond that time would mean death. But operation to be successful must be performed under perfect conditions by a highly skilled surgeon. These conditions were available on board the hospital ships at Scapa Flow but not on board our own ship where the Surgeon was suffering from lack of practice and the aseptic conditions were bound to be doubtful. Which was fairer to the patient. the risk of unskilled treatment or the danger of the time factor? As far as I knew we were at least twenty-four hours from our base. It was a terrible dilemma.

I took it straight to our Captain and explained everything. I was quite prepared to operate within twelve hours. He listened as usual with his grave sympathy and acute appreciation of the difficulties. Then he ordered the Engineer Commander and the Navigator to be called, and I listened while they discussed whether it was possible to arrive within the time I considered the limit. The Navigator turned to his charts and ruled off the course and gave the distance. The Captain looked doubtful and half shook his head; but the Engineer Commander gave his funny little half smile and nod, and I knew the boy was saved.

'We are due for a full speed trial anyway,' he said to the Captain, and turning to me added, 'You had better communicate with the hospital ship to have everything ready as soon as we arrive.'

Even as I left the bridge to go below and look after my patient I could tell by the mighty throb that we were gathering speed. Hour after hour we accelerated, and the stokers down below who had got wind of the need for haste strove as they had never done before even in action. Standing below the bridge in the dawn when we had worked up to nearly 34 knots, I wondered that anything made by man could stand such a strain and began to panic whether our engines were likely to break down. It had happened often enough before in other ships and I could see no good reason why we should be exempt.

Worried to death by the anxiety of it I went below and met the Engineer Commander stepping out of one of the engine room hoists. He asked me what was the matter, and I blurted out my fears. Again came the funny little half smile full of confidence, and before it, it was impossible to panic any longer. 'She's all right,' he answered.

She was. At an estimated cost of £700 he had pushed the gigantic mass of the ship over 300 miles in under ten hours. The lad was taken to the hospital ship, operated upon, and tucked comfortably away in bed before 2 o'clock. Next day he was swearing at the sisters and doctors for not giving him enough to eat. After seeing the operation skilfully and swiftly performed I went back to the ship and went into the Engineer Commander's cabin to thank him for saving the boy's life. He was so busy getting a perfect polish on his finger nails that he could only spare me a little nod.

Of the other officers on board I can only give fleeting glimpses. The junior medical officers, shot suddenly by a burst of burning enthusiasm into the deadly monotony of our sea warfare with its limited opportunities for professional work, its boring occupations of decoding, grummet making, sampling air specimens and dissecting the curious mental attitude of the bluejacket towards his authorised healer, found the life on board difficult in the extreme. One of them, who was a brilliant young physician attached to a large hospital, complained bitterly to me that one of the men had asked for treatment until such time as he could consult his 'proper doctor.' When pressed to give the name of the 'proper doctor' the patient admitted that he did not know it but 'everybody knew 'im. He was a chemist in the 'Igh Street in Portsmouth.' Finally this medical officer got so tired of the life that he applied for, and after much difficulty received, permission to exchange into the Army, where he lasted about three months. But previous to his departure he had done the bravest act of which I had personal cognisance during the War. During a lull in action I had called for a volunteer ambulance party to travel over an exposed part of the ship to remove an officer and some men from a turret which had been struck by a shell. A renewal of the action, which might take place at any moment, would have meant certain death for the party. The reply of our race to a call such as this whether in peace or war is invariably the same, a selflessness and disregard for danger whose heroism lies in the fact that it is the very antithesis of heroics. The little party under the medical officer returned safely with their job perfectly accomplished, and the only nervousness displayed was by myself who had sent them. The other medical officer was later appointed to a patrol ship which was torpedoed and sunk by a submarine in the approaches to the Firth of Clyde. Whilst the ship was sinking he was busy bringing up his helpless sick to the upper deck, and the last seen of him was when he went below, in spite of warnings, to complete the duty entrusted to him. Rescue for him would have been a certainty if he had been willing to abandon his sick to their fate. It is good to have lived and worked with such men.

On one occasion one of the medical officers reported that in making a surprise visit to the sick bay he had found the Chief Petty Officer drunk. This C.P.O. was an excellent man in every way, and his defection was a serious source of anxiety to me. He was brought before the Captain, and on my strong representation he was lightly dealt with but was warned that any repetition of the offence would entail the dipping of his rate. As his replacement would have been, for some time at any rate, a blow to the efficiency of my department it was up to us to see that the offence was not repeated.

The first question to be settled was the source of the alcohol. As he had charge of the medical stores it was possible that he had been broaching; but a careful checking showed there was no shortage, and the checking hurt. the C.P.O.'s feelings terribly. He protested that I ought to have known him better than to suggest he was capable of such dereliction of duty, but still stubbornly refused to indicate the source of his supply. The 'three water' grog issued as his rum ration could not have caused intoxication, and I was completely puzzled. Among our younger men it is rare for the rum ration to be drawn, as they prefer the money allowance in lieu. Our Paymaster finally gave me the cue when discussing the matter with him, as he told me that all of my sick berth staff – six of them – drew their rum ration. Five minutes cross-examination of each of them separately solved the problem. The Chief Petty Officer had compelled all of them to draw their rum rations and then present them to him, which, with his own share, represented nearly half a bottle of rum. The supply was easily stopped and thereafter I had nothing to blame and much to praise.

Looking back is like sitting in a darkened cinema and watching a film being flashed at top speed across the screen. Now and then a slow motion picture appears and it is possible to examine in detail the life we led and some of the actors. One of them – must there always be one such even in a community such as ours? – brought sorrow and disgrace to his parents and dishonour to the ship on board which he served.

Never can I forget his tortured face as he stood on the quarter-deck, a thing apart, and with bared head listened to the sentence which stripped him of his uniform and cast him forth from the comity of honourable men to bury his shame in the mud of Passchendaele.

If sometimes during the years when we rubbed shoulders together we jostled one another a bit roughly it is completely forgotten, and nothing remains except the intense loyalty of everyone to the ship and the Service which brought us together. Of our fellows who died it is but fitting to say that their fate was accepted as the common lot that might befall any of us, and with that knowledge we lived and fought for our country, full of pride in the ideal which had brought her into the War. Our attitude towards the enemy was one of respect for a brave and determined opponent who, in our opinion, was grievously misguided in his political outlook.

Chapter V
Scarborough

Our outbreak of tonsillitis was beginning to weigh heavily on the efficiency of the ship when we received orders to join the main Fleet at Scapa Flow. This time we gave all coasts, and especially headlands, a wide berth in case of minefields, but we had to approach the coast as we neared the Pentland Firth, which we did during the night. Luckily for our Fleet the conditions for laying minefields round about the southern entrance to the Flow – the one usually taken by our ships – were the worst possible on account of the great depths and terrific tides. Of course all lighthouses in the Pentland Firth had been extinguished during the War, but we had made signals asking that they should be lit about the time we were due, and it was rather startling to see a lighthouse suddenly show its rays in the darkness and then as suddenly be extinguished as we passed.

We made the entrance to the Flow without difficulty and it was interesting on a visit two years later to see the elaborate protections of this entrance compared with those when we first entered. On this occasion there were none, whilst on the second there were, as far as I remember, three 'gates' which had to be opened before we could pass through. The 'gate' was a narrow opening between two drifters which supported a heavy wire net between them. On the shore side of each drifter was another net which effectually blocked the passage to submarines.

Of course there were constant rumours and occasional actual submarine attacks. In one case a drifter had driven a submarine under so that she was blind, and when she pushed her periscope above the surface once more she was close against the drifter's side. She immediately submerged again before the drifter could do anything, but as she went down the engineer of the drifter hit the periscope a blow with a sledge hammer and so damaged her that the submarine had to come to the surface, and her crew were taken off; but, of course, they had opened their ship's seacocks and she sank before she could be captured. Later in the War the submarine would have been dealt with by a depth charge; but that method of attack was still in the future.

On another occasion a submarine had been driven under near the entrance to the Flow but in close proximity to the Lother Reef. This reef is chiefly dangerous from the fact that it is submerged, and the tidal current sometimes runs at the rate of 9 knots over it, so that the level of the water may be 3 feet higher on the weather than on the lee side. The submarine being blind could not know what the current was doing to her, and finally those chasing her saw her rolled over the reef by the pressure of the tide.

Scapa Flow is an enormous inland sea with numerous bays and islands scattered over it. There are three entrances, the western narrow and twisting, the eastern shallow and almost useless for ships of war, and the southern wide, deep, and easily approached apart from the tempestuous races of the Pentland Firth. The eastern entrance had been closed by the sinking of merchant ships across it. On arrival we were astonished to find that even our huge fleet of battleships, battle cruisers, light cruisers, destroyers and numberless auxiliaries only occupied a very small part of the Flow, so small in fact that a story may be told to illustrate it. One evening early in the War there was a buzz that a submarine had managed to get into the Flow, and there was the usual flap. Its entrance seemed to be pretty well authenticated and all the ships got under way, as to remain at anchor was to provide an easy target. All, that is to say, except the flagship. The Admiral was giving a dinner party and had no intention of having it disturbed. So orders were given that the fleet should circle round the flagship, which they did until the dinner party was over and the flap had died down.

As there seemed to be a certain degree of stagnation in the sea war, I went, with the Captain's permission, on board the flagship to see whether we could take over one of the auxiliaries for hulking purposes, so that we could get rid of part of the crew and have their quarters on board thoroughly hogged out and disinfected. The Secretary indicated a ship which he thought might be suitable, so away I went in the picket boat to talk the matter over with her captain. As I neared her she proved to be a fine big ship of about 6,000 tons, and I thought I had found a prize. A weary-faced elderly man in uniform met me at the top of the ladder and took me to his big comfortable cabin under the forebridge. My errand explained to him, he stared at me in a puzzled way.

'But you can't hulk men on board me. It's impossible!'

'Impossible? Why?'

'Because I'm a frozen meat ship with insulated holds, and I'm four-fifths full of frozen mutton.'

'Let me have a look.'

'Certainly.'

The ship was useless for my purposes and I made a move to go.

'For God's sake, man, stay and have a cup of tea with me. You're the first person I've spoken to since the boarding officer brought me in two months ago.'

We sat down to tea, of which the Captain took little. Impelled by curiosity I asked him:

'What are you doing here?'

'What am I doing here?' He jumped off his seat and began striding rapidly backwards and forwards across his cabin, whilst the words full of pent-up bitterness poured from him. 'That's what I'm asking myself night and day, morning and evening, every minute of the time while I sit here and do nothing. I don't know what I'm doing here. We got into Liverpool the day after war broke out and had just started unloading our cargo when a naval officer came down and told us to stop discharging. "You are to proceed at once to Scapa Flow and report yourself to the Commander-in-Chief." "Fine," thinks I, "they want my mutton. Here's a chance of doing something!" So I came up here and they pointed out this billet to me and told me to moor. And except for the postman from the flagship, and the dumping on me of some pieces of unwanted furniture; not a single soul has been near me since then. When I saw an officer coming alongside today, "At last!" I thought; "here's a job for me at last!" And my mutton's going bad, 5,000 tons of it – it won't keep for ever in the holds of these ships. And finally I know what they'll do. There'll be another submarine panic and they'll take and sink me across one of the entrances just as they did with these poor fellows.' He jerked his hand towards the melancholy evidence of the truth of his fears. 'And that's a fine end after forty years at sea!'

We who were in the forefront of the fighting line often failed to realise the bitterness of soul which racked the peace of hundreds of capable, clever, energetic and brave men who were compelled by the war to undergo the dull routine of apparently useless duty. It was my fortune to meet it on several occasions when there was nothing I could do to help or comfort. They were doing their bit, it was true, but a divine discontent with the futility of their bit when they knew they were capable of so much better things was not to be wondered at. I said what I could and left him after promising to look him up for a yarn at some other time. But our stay in Scapa was short and there was much to do. We were having trouble with our rangefinders, which there seemed some difficulty in correcting, and we were constantly cruising about inside the Flow for their adjustment, and for aiming tube practice with our guns. Finally we were ordered to Invergordon for battle practice and I never saw him again.

Having got rid of our more serious invalids to the hospital ships we left. Nor were any of us sorry, I believe. The winter time at Scapa with the short days and long dark nights, lying off heathercovered islands with not a tree and only a crofter shieling to look at, had a most depressing effect on everybody. For reasons already given the Germans had not been able to mine the entrances to Scapa, but our other northern base, Cromarty Firth, was a comparatively easy job. So they had done it and it was a good well-laid minefield but quite useless for its original object, like much German work. Once we had mapped out its area it was a godsend to our Fleet, and we took full advantage of it. Running between it and the shore we could fire over it out to sea at any range we liked, as within its perfect shelter no submarine dare approach.

So we did our one and only big gun firing and were then swept into the fiasco of the Scarborough raid.

* * *

A bitter winter's afternoon and signals passing rapidly from the flagship round the Fleet. 'Steam at two hours' notice.' That is the warning announcement and it is made frequently enough, so that it raises little more than our eyebrows in anticipation. Soon we know it will be followed by either a shortening of the time or a reversion to our usual war routine of 'Steam at four hours' notice.' Which it is to be on this occasion we have, of course, no idea. It all depends on the news from our Intelligence Department, which is the constant marvel of us all. Not one enemy ship seems to be able to move across their docks without our people knowing of it beforehand or just as it is taking place. And any suspicious movement of the enemy Fleet is immediately reflected in increased activity on our part. Steam at two hours' notice means nothing definite. It is just the uneasy growling of the watch-dog which hears strange footsteps in the distance.

'Steam for full speed at 17.30.' The watch-dog is up and with ears cocked listens to the footsteps coming nearer. Soon there is all the bustle of departure. The boats have already been hoisted on board and now there is the clank of cables through the hawseholes and down the sparling pipes as the ship is unmoored and the great anchors weighed. There is no doubt about one thing – we are going to sea to-night. 'The Hun must be out. Coastal raid, I suppose,' mutters somebody in the brilliantly lighted wardroom, 'Hope to catch them this time.'

Out into the wild North Sea on a December night, we leave our base at Invergordon, move cautiously and carefully down the narrow Cromarty Firth, and then, with the Soutars astern, begin working up to full speed. There is evidently something more than a flap this time with this apparent need for haste, but all we can learn from the decoding room is that some of the enemy battle cruisers are at sea, apparently with the object of making a raid on some of the north-east coast towns. 'Fortified towns' as the enemy calls them when one of his chance shells happens to kill a soldier home on leave. 'He won't catch us napping this time as he did at Yarmouth' we say; but we have a long way to go before we can be in one of the likely areas. The chances too are all in favour of the enemy when it comes to a tip and run raid. He knows exactly where he is going and we don't. We have to guess that from the wireless reports to the Admiralty from our patrols.

These give the enemy's position when sighted and the course he was steering, and when the different reports have been collated and checked they give some idea of his general scheme. From these his destination will be guessed and the information passed on to us. This is all a work of time and there is little time to spare, since with a bare hour's start the enemy can be under the shelter of the guns of Heligoland before our pursuing vessels can bring him to action. Of course he will lay mines as he nears our coast, hoping that we shall blunder in amongst them, and the subsequent confusion and uncertainty will also help him in making good his escape. There are many possibilities and there are only two things of which we can be certain; one, that he will try to avoid action, and the other that we shall make him fight if we can.

Unfortunately the chances against the defending force intercepting one of these raids are very great. Although the reported course of the attackers may give the impression that certain towns are his objective they may at any moment alter these courses and so deceive the defenders' patrols. Thus it might be assumed that they intended to attack the Hartlepools. If the Fleet gathered off these towns so as to ward off the attack they might find too late that another town many miles away was the real objective. It may be taken as axiomatic that only battle cruisers have sufficient speed and armament to attack battle cruisers, and as our superiority over the enemy in that class of ship is very small we cannot divide our Fleet up so as to protect any possible town along a coastline of 300 miles from attack. What we always hoped for was that we would receive notice of the bombardment in time to prevent their return altogether or do them so much damage that they would give the game up as not being worth the losses incurred. It should be remarked that the only value of these coastal raids to the enemy was the possible moral effect on the British nation. They did have a moral effect, but it was precisely the opposite of what the enemy hoped for as they found the raids stiffened our backs instead of weakening them. The military value of these raids to the enemy was just – nothing.

What is our Fleet going to do, then? We may be lucky and find that we are just to seaward of the enemy when he attacks the coast town. His speed is such that if our light cruisers or destroyers get in touch with him he can run away from any of our battleships, and his power is so great that our smaller craft must keep out of range until the battle cruisers come up. At modern ranges that is a distance of about 10 miles, if the visibility is reasonably good. As for mines, which he will undoubtedly lay, there is no time to search for them by sweeping in the usual manner and their minefield will be located only by a ship stumbling on it and exploding one. That risk must be run by the smaller craft. All we can do is to lie off the coast clear of the probable minefield area and in such a position, if we can find it, fetch them up with a round turn.

As luck would have it, on this occasion the battle cruisers are not at full strength, as two have been detached to attend to a little affair at the Falkland Islands and another is away on special service. The German of course knows about this shortage and he is counting on it for the success of his present attack. So the battle cruisers must keep together or they will be crushed piece-meal by the stronger fleet. It is true we have the Fifth Battle Squadron to back us up; but although the ships are powerful enough to smash the enemy, it must meet him, as these battleships have not got the speed to chase him successfully. Unless we can manage to hold the enemy up, the main fleet cannot arrive from Scapa in time to take any part.

There is little sleep for anyone on board our ships that night as they hurtle through the darkness against the rising wind, sea and rain. When one remembers that these huge vessels are driving along at 26 knots in utter and complete darkness, since no navigation lights are shown and the whole interior lighting is so screened that not a chink can be seen anywhere, that each ship is only two cables or 400 yards astern of its dimly seen next ahead, the strain on the officers on the bridge can be faintly imagined. The officers chiefly responsible for the station keeping are the Captain, the Navigating Commander and the Officer of the Watch. In the engine room an engineer officer stands on the control platform ready to obey on the instant the signals from the bridge for more or less speed. The two last officers will get their reliefs at the end of their four-hour watch, but for the others no such let-up can be hoped for until the clearing of the weather or the first streaks of dawn come to give them a little respite.

Should the weather become thick so that the next ahead is no longer visible she will tow a fogbuoy – a small white buoy at the end of two cables of light wire rope – and the whole of the bridge's efforts will be concentrated on keeping that leaping, splashing object just a little on one or other bow. In case of fog the next ahead will also probably burn her after searchlight, so focussed that the beam will play on the bows of the ship astern. It is a weird sensation dashing through the murk with nothing but a hazy beam of light on your forecastle head and a splash in the water to tell you that 30,000 tons of ship are only 400 yards away from you.

Speed must be maintained exactly, so as to keep correct station in the line. On the least sign of faltering or slowing down of the next ahead, the officer of the watch must be prepared to give orders to the quartermaster at the wheel to go to port or starboard, so that she may swing out of line a little in case she overruns her consort. Nor must the ship be allowed to slacken speed so as to confuse her next astern. Then a message must be sent to the engine room to send the ship along faster or slower as may be necessary. It takes an

1. *Tiger* at Roysth, 1914.

2. HMS *Tiger*, showing alterations made after the war.

3. A direct hit on a turret (HMS *Tiger*).

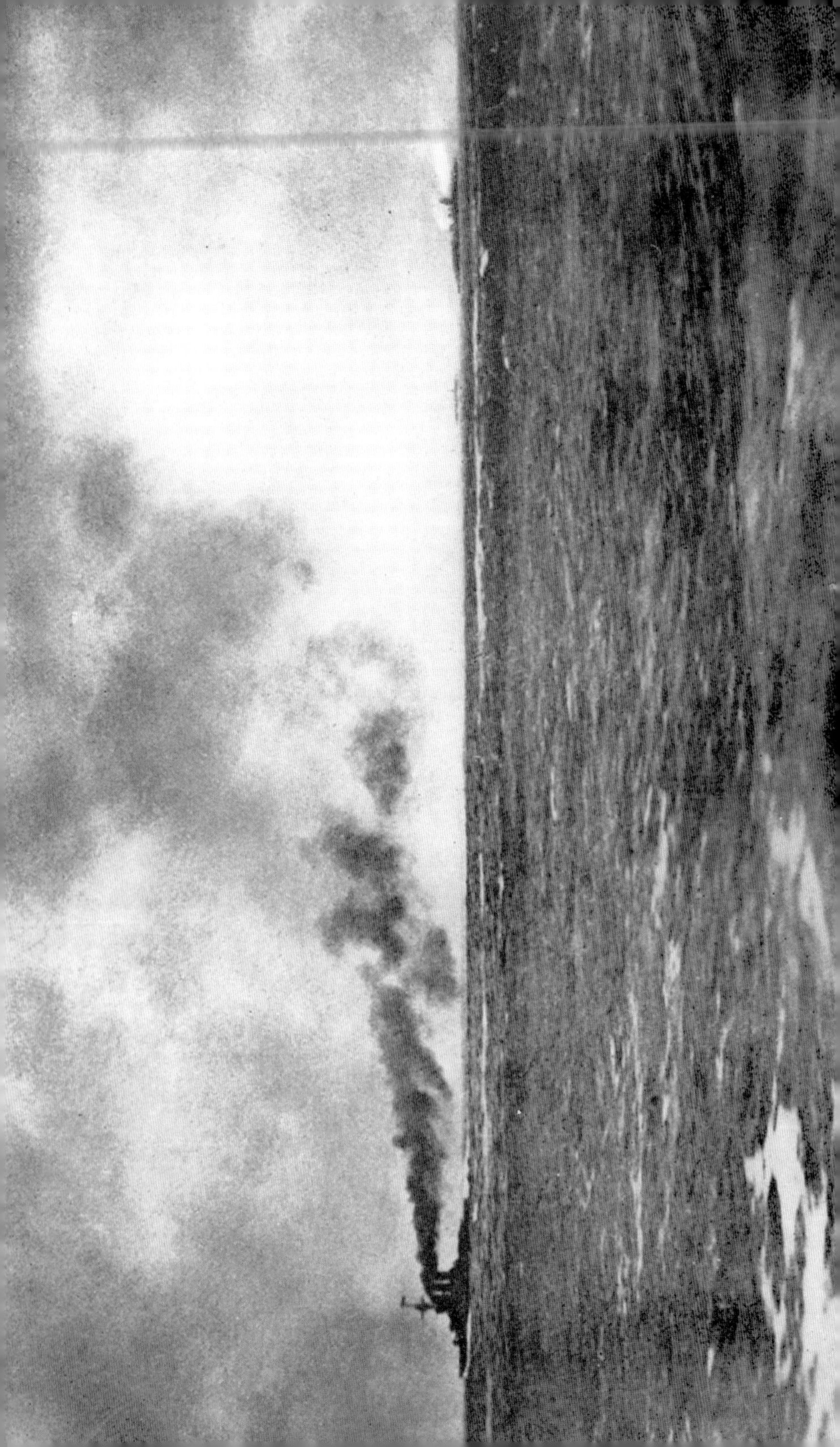

4. (*Left*) *Tiger* in action (Jutland, 31st May, 1916).
5. (*Above*) The last of the *Queen Mary*, 31st May, 1916.

6. The writer.

7. The wreck of the *Invincible*, 31st May, 1916.

8. A direct hit on an armour plate (HMS *Tiger*).

appreciable time in that wind, sea and darkness to be sure you are coming up on your leader; an appreciable time to give the orders to the man at the wheel and the midshipman at the engine room telegraph or voice tube; an appreciable time for these orders to reach the various brains they are meant for; an appreciable time for these orders to be faultlessly translated into action; an appreciable time for the ship to respond to the various controls. As the space between the two ships in terms of time is only thirty seconds if the ship ahead should suddenly break down, one can comprehend the terrible strain on the men who are responsible to the nation for the safety of 1500 men and £4,000,000 worth of property.

Dawn comes late on this December morning, with a troublesome sea, driving rain and a lowering sky which promises worse weather to come. Early we hear from the wireless signals coming through that our light cruisers and destroyers are in touch with the enemy's screen of small craft. A merchant ship has struck a minefield laid parallel with the coast off Scarborough. There is an older minefield also laid by the enemy to the north of this and there is a gap between the two. Then signals come in thick; Scarborough is being shelled by the enemy battle cruisers. Then we hear the Hartlepools are being shelled. Just time to fling a few shells ashore and then back to sea again, trusting to their heels.

But in the meantime we have located the extent of their minefield and we know the position and exact width of the gap through which they must pass before they can gain the open sea. The gap is a wide one, some 20 miles or so, much too wide for a day like this. But full of hope the Fifth Battle Squadron is strung seaward from the southern edge of the gap and the battle cruisers from the northward edge. Even here we are not altogether safe from mines, and the day of the paravane is not yet, so we dare not close the shore. But they are coming along at last and heading straight for the trap we have laid for them, for the patrol has signalled that she is engaged with the enemy – a mosquito fighting an ironclad. Our hopes were high and justifiably so, for our dispositions were perfect, the enemy must pass through the lane between the battleships and battle cruisers, and our combined strength was overwhelming. The bugle sounded for action stations and we went to our billets convinced that this time there would be no cry of 'What is our Navy doing?'

And then – down came the threatened gale of wind and rain. The storm-tossed sea was driven in masses of spoondrift across our decks until our hulls were barely visible to the men in the tops. In that fearful riot of storm visibility absolutely disappeared; we could not guess at the positions of our next ahead or astern as we drove through the welter of sea and rain, whilst the storm clouds seemed to graze our trucks. A surging sound heard even through the clamour of the gale called attention to our port side, where one of our own destroyer leaders, supposed to be acting as a screen half a mile away on our beam, was almost rubbing alongside. We depended on visibility of some kind for success. There was no visibility. Fight? We could do nothing, nothing.

So they passed through the lane unharmed and when the squall had lifted sufficiently to allow the normal employment of the ship to be resumed, they were beyond pursuit. The Fifth Battle Squadron is supposed to have had a glimpse of them between squalls, but was unable to recognise them with any certainty as friend or foe. From positions plotted out afterwards it was certain that it could not have been us that the battleships caught sight of; but in that murk a mistake was easy. Yet his failure broke the Admiral's heart and in the church at Rye may be seen the monument to his memory.

Soon signals were coming through from the Admiralty wireless. 'Enemy battle cruisers sighted in such and such a position steering east.' As the swiftest of our ships, we were detailed to follow in chase of one of them, the *Roon*, which was supposed to be lagging behind the faster ships. We followed for an hour or so but were recalled to the main fleet by a signal saying that the enemy had been sighted in such a position that pursuit was hopeless. Shortly after rejoining we were all ordered back to our bases.

Our Engineer Lieutenant came up to the wardroom and looked round.

'Well, I've brought you here. I suppose I shall have to take you back again.'

Nobody answered.

* * *

The lesson of the Scarborough raid was that our ships were too far away from the threatened northeastern coasts, and three or four days after our return, the battle cruisers were ordered to be based on Rosyth, and here we remained until the end of the war. Every mother's son and, what was probably more important, every mother's daughter in the huge population of Edinburgh and Leith and all the surrounding towns knew exactly where and what we were, but still the censor was not allowed to pass such information in letters from the Fleet. So if you were a conscientious soul, you got a friend on shore to write to your relations to come and see you. Otherwise you posted the letter on shore yourself.

Life on board whilst we were based on Rosyth was much pleasanter than at Scapa or Invergordon. Socially we were made much of, although we were usually somewhat taken aback by the invariable suggestion of our hostesses that we might like to have a bath. I hope our appearance did not always justify the kindly thought.

With the recent memory of the Scarborough raid still strong upon the minds of the Admiralty there were many of what we used to call 'panics.' Usually the orders were for steam at four hours' notice, and then officers and certain of the ship's company were allowed shore leave from 1 to 5 p.m. If the notice were shortened to two hours or less a 'panic' was on and no leave was granted. During the four hours' leave it was easy to get up to Edinburgh. Occasionally the notice was shortened to two hours after we had gone on leave, and then, as you sat in an Edinburgh cafe or cinema, or wandered along Princes Street, an unknown individual would suddenly appear at your elbow from nowhere in particular and whisper 'Return to your ship, Sir!' In half an hour Princes Street, which had been alive with naval uniforms, would be deserted – an excellent method of informing all and sundry that the Fleet was about to proceed on its business. So marked was this sudden flight that if you had been calling on a friend and saw nobody in the street when you came out you immediately went back to your ship. Of course, if you were going anywhere other than the usual haunts of the naval officer, you were expected to tell one of your shipmates, so that he could communicate with you at once should the warning be given. People in Edinburgh used to say that once the naval officers left Princes Street the only men seen were soldiers and German submarine officers, who used to land at Dunbar and come up to town to allay the tedium of their patrol.

We were still being 'completed' and there was almost always a gang of dockyard workmen on board. By this time the price of labour was approaching fantastic heights as measured by the pre-war standpoint, and the wages paid to these workmen was a sore point with the bluejacket, who on his 1s. 9d. a day was expected to provide his uniform, pay his extra messbill, keep his wife and children at home, buy his 'bacca' and have something left over for an occasional gamble at 'crown and anchor.' The argument of course was that he need not stick at 1s. 9d. a day, but few ships in H.M. Service are manned throughout by Petty Officers and Leading Rates. If the ship went to sea in a hurry Jack still drew his 1s. 9d. a day; but the mechanics also drew an allowance known as 'danger money' which came to 6s. a day. This 'danger money' stuck in Jack's gizzard, and not all the arguments of the free born, enlightened Union men could force the unsavoury bolus down his throat.

Chapter VI
The Dogger

If the raid on Scarborough has done nothing else it has taught us that the disposition of the Fleet, with the battleships at Scapa and the battle cruisers based on Invergordon, is susceptible of improvement. In a few days after the raid the battle cruisers received orders that in future they were to be based on the Firth of Forth. As we had still no submarine defence we had to lie above the Forth Bridge.

The new base of course has its advantages and disadvantages, the one being practical and the other theoretical. In view of the possibility of further coastal raids, the base at Rosyth is about 120 miles nearer in space and about six hours nearer in time to the north-east coast towns. The defence against submarine attack, thanks to the Forth Bridge, can be developed much more easily and quickly. Under our lee we have the dockyard at Rosyth, a much more efficient repair shop than the floating dock temporarily moored at Invergordon.

Against the base is the possibility that submarine attack may be easier in the entrance to the Forth and mine laying could probably be more readily indulged in. There was always a chance that an enemy agent might be able to blow the bridge up and, for a time at any rate, effectually bottle up the cruisers which moored above the bridge. There was also the question of spies. These could be readily dealt with if discovered in a small Highland village, but the enormous population in the many towns round about our base could shelter a regiment of spies easily and they would have little difficulty in learning our movements, which, except at night-time, were plain to everybody who took the trouble to look.

As far as we knew none of the theoretical objections to the base ever materialised, while the advantages increased as the War dragged on. From the ships' companies' standpoint the change was pure gain. What little leave was granted to us was spent under infinitely happier conditions, climatically and socially, than those that prevailed in the northern bases. During our first fortnight or so at the new base nothing much happened and we spent the time mostly in making grommets for the army ammunition depots. Not a soul-stirring occupation, but it helped to pass the time and gave us the feeling that we were helping just a little.

We were startled after dark on the evening of the 18th January by the order to prepare for sea and raise steam for full speed at once. That means unmooring ship and, dark as it is by 5 p.m., the group lights on the forecastle head show the clanking cable being brought up through the hawse-holes so as to get the swivel off. As it is removed, away goes the cable with a rush and, writhing like a snake in the semi-darkness, it strikes with all its force at the left leg of our boatswain who has been standing too near it. With a groan the injured man drops on the deck, and the first lieutenant who is in charge of the unmooring shouts for a medical officer to come at once. He hastily arrives on the scene and in a trice makes his diagnosis and reports.

'Compound fracture of the leg. Unfit to go to sea. Must be sent to hospital.'

'Make a signal for the Hospital boat to come alongside at once,' orders the Captain.

The injured man is carefully and skilfully carried to one side so that the work of unmooring need not be interrupted; the broken limb is dressed and lashed up in temporary splints.

The ship cannot wait, and if the Hospital boat does not arrive in time the patient must take his chance at sea. But soon the boat is alongside and the patient, who has been placed in a cot, is lowered gently into it. Meanwhile the unmooring is completed, the anchors are weighed, and close astern of her monster flagship the *Lion*, the ship proceeds to sea. Nothing can be seen of the ship ahead except a dark grey mass on the waters with a tiny electric bulb at the extreme stern so shaded that only its reflection from the tumbling waters of the wake is visible. Once clear of the narrow waters even that feeble illumination will be dowsed.

On deck all is darkness and quiet. Occasionally you may hear a smothered curse as a shadowy ill-defined figure makes violent contact with an unseen obstacle. Overhead are neither moon, stars, nor sky, only the darker shadow of the cloud of smoke from our three funnels driving wildly athwart a lighter background which is the zenith. Below in the wardroom it is light and cheery enough, but every crevice from which a chink of light might betray our presence to a lurking enemy in the darkness outside is carefully blocked. Luckily our tinned air system is working perfectly, so that we can breathe easily and happily in the confined space.

'What's the stunt this time?' asks the senior engineer as he chews at the end of an unusually long cigarette holder. There is rarely a cigarette in this holder and when he gets excited it is only betrayed by the slow up and down motion of the outer end.

'Don't know,' says someone. 'Coastal raid, I expect.'

'Well, see you catch 'em this time,' says the engineer. 'I'm tired of taking you people there and back again just for the fun of it.' He is a man who has perfect confidence in his engines and Shakespeare's dictum about fat men, but in precious little else.

'We'll catch 'em all right, old cock; never fear!' chimes in a lieutenant.

'No more of your Scarborough tricks, anyhow,' growls the engineer. 'The British public that pays you at the cost of its beer money won't stand for it twice, and it bores me stiff.'

But Scarborough is still a sore subject with us and the discussion drops.

Someone comes up from the decoding room where he has been busy for the last two hours decoding the cypher messages which are constantly coming in. We have a theory on board that the Admiralty stick to cypher signals because they are more easily understood by the German than plain English. And we have an equally intimate knowledge of the German cyphers, which all helps to make things more interesting. The decoder is immediately assaulted for news, but, of course, he is under orders that he must communicate messages to no unauthorised person, not even his messmates. Not that it would make any difference if he did, but like 'Dora' ashore these regulations are good for your soul if not of any other value.

'Want me to be shot at dawn, you fellows, for betraying official secrets? But I don't mind telling you because I know the signal is just being handed round that the German battle cruisers are out.'

A chart is placed on the wardroom table and we crowd together over it. Hasty calculations are made as to speed and distances, and somebody calculates we ought to pick them up at daylight.

'Daylight!' says the engineer. 'When's daylight? I haven't seen daylight for a week.'

And daylight it was. At 7.30 next morning a group of officers standing on the platform beneath the bridge saw, as the grey streaks of dawn showed pale against the eastern horizon, half a dozen columns of smoke, under which, but still invisible, were the German cruisers. They had already discovered us and, all hope of a raid abandoned, were scurrying as fast as their propellers could drive them back to their bases. We were obviously gaining on them as their speed was limited to that of their slowest ship, the *Blücher*, and by 9 o'clock we had raised them enough to recognise the *Derfflinger*, *Moltke*, and *Seydlitz*, with the smaller *Blücher* even then beginning to drop astern. The latter ship had nothing like the speed or fighting power of the others, which were evidently prepared to throw her to the wolves rather than peril their chance of escape.

We are in much the same predicament. Our ship is the fastest in the Fleet, but must keep astern of the Flagship which is only capable of about 27 knots, although her stokers are labouring to get the last ounce of steam out of her. Astern of us the *Princess Royal* cannot keep up the pace and is beginning to lag a bit, whilst the other division, headed by the *New Zealand*, will soon be hopelessly out of it. If only we had the *Queen Mary* with us to even things up a bit, for that fleeing trio should be more than a match for the two of us if they would only turn and fight. They still run, but as long as their speed is governed by the *Blücher*'s we can easily overhaul them before they get under the guns of Heligoland.

And now at 18,000 yards our guns begin to speak, and we concentrate on the doomed *Blücher* as the nearest target. She is struck again and again and gradually begins to lose speed, heel and get out of control. We leave her for our other slower ships to finish, which they will soon do, aye, and would rescue her drowning crew as well if it were not for that damned zeppelin and aeroplane raining bombs on the men who have forgotten warfare in their efforts at saving life at sea. But seemingly so mordant is the German's hate that he will kill one Englishman even should it entail the slaughter of three of his fellow countrymen.

Now having got rid of their lame duck the others can get on with their flight unhampered, and an increase of speed until it is equal to ours is at once worked up. We concentrate on the *Seydlitz*, and a lucky salvo pushes the whole of her quarterdeck guns and turrets all over the side but leaves her armoured deck and the vital propeller shafts and steering gear under it untouched. The smoke from their funnels is belching in, huge clouds and nothing seems to stay them. Only the *Lion* and the *Tiger* are within range and these three ships, on paper at least, should be more than a match for us. Why don't they turn and fight? Are Heligoland and safety of so much importance that they dare not face an inferior force? Still, as we chase, our slower vessels are dropping astern. The *Princess Royal* can be seen labouring along in the distance, but only the smoke from their funnels tells the whereabouts of our Second Division.

But what is this? Smoke and steam escaping from the *Lion* and she is gently listing and rapidly losing speed as she swings away to starboard out of our course. Signals fly from the Admiral for a destroyer to come and take him on board so that he may continue in charge of the action; but our destroyer screen is a long way away and it will be some time before he can be transferred. Admiral on *New Zealand* is ordered to take charge of the action; but he is so far astern that he can have little knowledge of what is happening and we are crossing the North Sea at such a speed that action must be called off soon. At any rate there is still the *Tiger* left to steam and fight. One against three. Surely? if ever? they will turn now and give us a taste of their mettle.

But neither to support a friend nor to fight a foe, whatever the odds in their favour, will the German cruisers alter their homeward course a single hair's breadth to-day.

And now it is our turn; there is no other target. All three of them have been so far chiefly concentrating on the *Lion* and have left us comparatively undamaged. Now all three concentrate on us and we have no reason to doubt the excellence of their shooting. *Biff!* and B turret is out of action, with two men, killed and several wounded. But no, it is not out of action completely. It is only the port gun that is useless, and soon the dead are cleared away, the wounded attended to, and the starboard gun is firing again. But the loss of one of our big 13·5 guns leaves only seven to return the deadly' hail being sent over us by the enemy. *Biff!* and we are struck again, but this time it is on armour and the thick steel plate is spattered with concentric circles but keeps the projectile out. *Biff!* and a shell enters the signal distributing station and explodes there, spreading death and destruction amongst the messengers. *Biff!* and a shell hits us on the boat deck and sets fire to the motor launch which, thanks to a few gallons of petrol in the fuel tank, blazes merrily with huge clouds of smoke. Away fire parties and put it out, but it lasts long enough and looks important enough for the enemy to report that they had set us on fire and had no doubt they had destroyed us. Still we go on firing and still *Biff! Biff! Biff!* we are struck.

And then comes the warning cry that submarines have been sighted and it is very likely true, as we are within 80 miles of Heligoland and their vessels have had plenty of time to get within touch of us. The Admiral has boarded his destroyer and is following us fast, but no destroyer is going to overtake the *Tiger* today.

And then a wireless signal is handed in to us. 'Alter course N.E. and break off the engagement.' Hardly need for that yet, we think; but 'orders is orders.' One last salvo from us at the flying cruisers, one last biff from them, and we carry out our instructions.

How were we to know that the signals were incorrectly interpreted? Why should signal mistakes occur? It is 12.15

p.m. and we have been in action for over three hours – for the last hour we have been fighting them single-handed.

We quickly regain the Fleet and find the Admiral has been transferred to the *Princess Royal*. The *Lion* is soon come up with – a melancholy sight with her dangerous looking list and her complete inability to proceed under her own steam. She can only get back to Rosyth in one way and that is by towing. That is easy enough for our ships and soon she is astern of the *Indomitable* and the procession starts for home. This is a fine chance for an enemy submarine, as they can easily bag both tower and towed which can neither zigzag nor speed. No chances of such a disaster were taken and for eighteen hours the destroyers and cruisers circled round the tow until we were safe in home waters.

Next day from our anchorage above the bridge we watched the wounded *Lion* passing under it as she was towed to her billet.

'Coming home with the milk, I call it,' remarked our engineer lieutenant.

* * *

We had left Rosyth for the Dogger Action in a great hurry and carried with us some wiremen who were fixing up some electrical circuits. Their foreman was one of the worst type of argumentative workman, and on many occasions he had made himself objectionable to the ship's company by his criticism of what he said was their 'slavish' attitude towards their officers. When it was evident that an action was going to take place his men offered to help in any way they could and were immediately told off to jobs; but the foreman had decided that his Union would not approve of this and he refused to do anything. He strolled about the upper deck, and when the firing began took refuge in a six-inch gun casemate.

The action had been going on for some time and things were pretty bad in my corner of the ship, when I got a message from the casemate that a casualty was being sent down. I knew we hadn't been hit on that side of the ship and rather wondered what it was. By and by the Neil Robertson stretcher was opened up, and out on the floor rolled the foreman of wiremen. I have seen panic once and fear once, and I hope never to live to see them again. The first was frightsome, but this was simply loathsome and disgusting. He rolled on the floor in agony, shouting at me to stop the fighting, to tell the Captain that he was to be put on shore at once as his job was not fighting, invoking the wrath of his Union on each and all of us, cursing, moaning and sobbing.

Whilst the uproar was at its height and I was trying to find out whether he had been injured in any way, a horny old bluejacket who was nursing his wounds leant over the edge of his cot overhead. With a look of ineffable disgust he addressed the writhing heap on the floor.

'Oh! There ye are, are ye? Earning yer danger money, are yer? Well, I hopes yer widder draws it,' and then solemnly spat.

Having been unable to find any injury it was time to end the scene, so half a grain of morphia was injected into his upper arm, to the accompaniment of further objurgations and threats. In ten minutes he was sound asleep.

Our casualties were not very heavy, but they entailed a lot of work, and some thirty-six hours afterwards I was superintending their transfer to the hospital ship at Rosyth. As the last one was going over the side my steward came up to me and said,

'What shall we do with that foreman, Sir?'

'Good Lord! I had forgotten all about him. Where is he?'

'Still sound asleep in the Distributing Station.'

'All right! Roll him up in a blanket, put him in a cot, and send him with the others.'

And, as far as we were concerned, that was the end of him.

I did not see the sinking of the *Blücher* nor had I any desire to do so. The commercial acumen of the gentleman who exposed a film at the moment best fitted to illustrate her death agonies and then sold the film to a press agency was strongly and adversely criticised by many, who considered the action little to the credit of a naval officer. We still had our idealists who believed we were fighting a righteous war. It was our duty to do this sort of thing but not to gloat over it. The navigator of the *Blücher* was amongst the few who were picked up, and it was said that his first remark in the wardroom of the ship which rescued him was 'Now I shall be able to go and have a look at my estate in Scotland.' Certainly he bore a well known Scottish name.

We believed we had done well in the action. Assuredly we had taken the hardest knocks and suffered the heaviest casualty list when for over an hour we were the sole target of the three best German battle cruisers. The Germans themselves believed they had sunk us, as a fire in our upper deck looked to them like our complete destruction. We expected at least to be congratulated and made something of for our prowess in the latter part of the action. What was our wrath and disappointment to find that we were very much in the dirt-tub. Our shooting was rotten and we had fired at the wrong ships. We had misread and disobeyed signals. We had done everything wrong that was possible and it was entirely due to us that the German cruisers had got away.

The whole business was investigated by a Court of Enquiry. What the evidence and findings were at this court I do not know, but as the result of it changes were made in our officers, and these were angrily resented in every part of the ship. Cast into the furnace of war as we had been, with a semi-completed ship, a scratch crew, and balked, through circumstances, of the long period of training which had been the lot of the other ships, the wonder was not that we had done badly, but that we had done so well. The back of the work had been broken, by the overworked, careworn men whose turn it was now to be broken themselves.

The Director General sent for me to come and discuss our battle arrangements. He was fiercely and hostilely critical.

'Why didn't you bury your dead at sea?'

I said I had suggested it but the Captain had decided otherwise.

'Why didn't you make better arrangements for a mortuary?'

The reply was that I had done so but that a German shell had declined to approve. Both of us were new to fighting and it was years since he had served on board a ship, so that it was difficult to explain what had happened.

At the end of the stormy interview I reminded him of his promise of a few months before to help me towards the special promotion which meant everything to my future in the Service.

'I cannot do anything for you. It's no use my putting your name forward.'

'Why, Sir? What have I done wrong?'

'Your ship didn't shoot straight.'

I rose wearily. 'Well, Sir, I'm willing to take anything you choose to say about my own department, but I'm damned if I'm going to carry the ship's shooting on my shoulders. Anyhow, she is my ship and these people are my messmates, and if they have to go under I'm glad to be in their company.'

'You're a fool!'

I left.

Back to the Tyne where the ship was having her battle damages repaired. At Newcastle I found I had to wait a bit for my local train to South Shields, and so I strolled about on the platform. Recognising from my uniform that I was a servant of the public a fat woman straddled in front of me.

'Where does the train for Tynemouth start from?' The manner of her address was intolerably offensive.

'Indeed, Madam, I haven't the faintest notion,' and I made her my best bow.

'Another word of impudence from you, young man, and I'll report you to the station-master.'

Later, when I was seated in a first class compartment, I found my fat lady friend's face pushed flat against the window pane, full of amazement.

We only stayed a few days in the Tyne, but the kindness of everyone we met in that smoky area will not soon be forgotten. If the Admiralty had no illusions on the subject, the Tynesiders thought we were the heroes of the Dogger affair and treated us accordingly.

Our repairs completed, we went back to the Forth, to endure as best we could the tedium of the sixteen months that was to elapse before the battle of Jutland. There were of course the usual stunts, panics, sweeps and patrols. On one of these occasions we were patrolling off the island of Sylt – with what object I know not, although we believed the idea was to investigate the possibility of landing an invading party in that region. But all day long as we cruised about, we could see high up in the sky to the eastward, and occasionally hidden by clouds, a long silver pencil which was wirelessing all our movements to the enemy. Safe she seemed, but not too safe, for even as we watched her, a chance shot from a light cruiser was fired. Then, wonder upon wonder, she seemed to break in the middle, which sagged downwards, and she started slowly dropping into the sea. One of our destroyers picked up the survivors, and as she had no companions to drop bombs indiscriminately on friend and foe alike, as in the case of the *Blücher*, the rescue was easily carried out.

But the days and nights were intolerably dreary, though everything possible was done to keep up our enthusiasm and spirits. Added to our other treats were the social conditions under which our families and relatives were living on shore. The price of food and lodgings were rising everywhere, and living for our dependants was daily becoming more difficult. Although the ever-ravening man of labour was satisfied to the point of enrichment at the expense of the country, nothing was done to allay the rapid impoverishment of those who had only their lives and not their free labour to offer for the nation's need. Nothing was done – no! I am unjust; something was done. In the usual monthly order appeared the comforting statement that in view of the rise in the cost of living, the Admiralty had been pleased to increase the victualling allowance paid to officers and men by the sum of ½d. per day. The vicious sneer with which this handsome concession was greeted should have struck a warning note. The men's letters to their wives and relatives were beginning to transgress the limit of 'Statements calculated to bring the Service into disrepute' and, as censor, it was difficult to know when to step in and interfere. Finally I had to send for a leading seaman one day, as it was impossible to pass his letter to his wife, contravening as it did the regulation just quoted. He came to me at the censor's office; a fine specimen of our best type of seaman, but sullen, hard-mouthed and with anxious eyes.

'I'm sorry I cannot allow this letter to be forwarded and I must warn you that if you continue to write statements like these you will get into trouble.'

He stared defiantly at me for a moment and then stood stock still at attention, looking straight to his front but made no reply. I thought rapidly for a minute.

'Tell me as a friend. What is the matter?'

He suddenly altered his attitude, gazed fixedly at me for a second, recognised, I hope, the real friendliness behind the officer's uniform, turned up the seaman's cap which he had been swinging to and fro in his left hand, produced a letter from the inside of the crown and handed it to me.

'Read that, Sir. That's what's the matter.'

'Shall I read it all?'

'Yes. Yes, Sir. Every word of it.'

There was very little in the letter that could not have been duplicated in every mess in the Fleet. His wife and child were starving and were being turned out of their house in Plymouth in favour of a munition worker who was going to pay more for rent alone than the seaman could possibly allot to his wife for all living purposes.

'Is she a Friendly Wife?' I asked, referring to that organisation by means of which officers' and men's wives kept in touch with one another and gave such assistance as was possible. It is not a charitable organisation but simply what the name implies.

'Yes, but they can't do anything for her. There are hundreds like her and the Friendly Wives have enough to do to look after widows and orphans.'

'Is there nothing else you can do?'

'I've tried everything, Sir. I've even tried to do "dobeying," but the other hands and the officers object to a leading rate doing that kind of work.' (It is not surprising that officers should object to a petty officer washing the dirty duds of the men he may be called upon to command.)

'No, you can't do dobeying,' I agreed.

'Then what else can I do, Sir?'

There was no answer. There could be no answer. The officers' wives were little better off. Before the war – I believe things have altered since – a rich officer was a rarity and there were few whose professional pay was not the major part of their income, and that pay was pitifully inadequate when the needs of wives and bairns had to be considered. The wives were cutting expenses as far as possible, shifting into yet cheaper and cheaper rooms in the dockyard towns, giving up the few luxuries they possessed and looking upon some necessities as luxuries. Marriage allowance was unknown and even in the Year of Grace 1936 is still denied to naval officers alone of all of those who sit in messes and serve His Majesty. A shame? Oh, yes! A shame! Even a First Lord of the Admiralty has admitted in Parliament that it is a shame, but to remove that shame was impossible as honourable conduct was so expensive.

A break was bound to come, and we whose hearts and ears were close to the hardly used men we loved and lived and fought with could only wonder what form the break would take.

It came. But, as befitted the service they belonged to, it was done decently, if not in order. On a certain day the battle cruisers received orders to proceed to sea and, as usual, the light cruisers which acted as a screen were to leave a little ahead of us. As the appointed time approached no movements were to be seen on the part of the light cruisers. After much signalling and secret messages we proceeded without them.

The rest I have to tell of this matter is rumour and as rumour it must be accepted. The men in the light cruisers had approached their officers and with the greatest respect, in accordance with the sympathetic bond they knew lay between them, informed them that until this question of pay was settled, they could not take the ships to sea. We heard this action spoken of as mutiny. Mutiny is an attempt at gaining the mastery of the ship. There was no such attempt and with our men there never could have been such an attempt.

There was a Court of Enquiry. Again I give rumour. Barge Goodenough rose in his wrath and swore that if ever men had reached breaking point, his had, that he did not condone their refusal of duty, but if justification could be possible the Admiralty had done their best to justify the men. David

THE DOGGER

Beatty, who had never known fear and despised favour, was even more emphatic in his denunciations, and the civilian officials who formed part of the Board cowered before the righteous indignation of these two men. And the reason we believed this rumour is because rumour, often a lying jade, so faithfully reflected the characters of these two men.

Anyhow the battle had been won for the men; but the war had to be over for nearly a year before tardy and inequitable justice was meted out to the officers by adopting, with severe cuts, the recommendations of the Jerram-Halsey committee.

Chapter VII
At Rosyth

A signal from the Flagship: – 'Flag to *Tiger*. His Majesty the King will visit and inspect the battle cruisers tomorrow. He will board your ship about 11 a.m. There is to be no formality.'

So, or in some such words, runs the message from the Admiral. It raises the ship's company to fever point of excitement and satisfaction, and impels everybody from the captain down to the latest joined boy to make a desperate effort at having everything in the ship, outside or inside, in a state of perfect readiness. Decks are scrubbed as if they had never been scrubbed before; brass is polished and re-polished; the mess decks are a snipe marsh and the bags and hammocks are still more neatly stowed in the racks; everywhere is hustle and preparation.

But the latter part of the signal causes some of us to chuckle. No formality! Whatever may be the King's attitude in barracks or on parade grounds we do not know and, truth to tell, care very little; but in a ship of war we know that this man has been accustomed to strip formality to shreds and unhesitatingly and with sure touch to lay bare whatever of efficiency or slackness it was meant to conceal. This was to be a real inspection and the officer or man who failed to come up to the high standard expected of him would have reason to blush until his dying day at the recollection of it.

Morning and the intense undercurrent of expectant happiness is felt like an electric current passing through the very structure of the ship herself. Everywhere the last unnecessary touches are being repeated over and over again to alleviate the mere tension of waiting.

Officers' Call! and we fall in on the quarterdeck whilst the Admiral's barge with the King on board comes alongside, the two bowmen holding their brightly polished brass boat-hooks aloft. Full speed astern! and the bowmen hook on to the guess warp and the barge stops dead alongside the bottom platform of the accommodation ladder. The midshipman in charge of the picket boat swings smartly round facing aft and salutes as the King steps on the platform and ascends the narrow ladder to the quarter-deck. The King halts momentarily in true naval fashion and returns the salute of the Captain and officer and then with a smile he shakes hands with the Captain. Not even the formal shrieking of the bosun's pipe marks the occasion and surely no King has ever boarded his ships with so little ceremony and so markedly as of one entering into his own kingdom. Talking to the Captain they both step aside a little whilst the accompanying staff tumble up the ship's side from the barge and take their places nearby. Only half a dozen men, this staff, but bearing names to conjure with in any naval service. A few minutes of conversation with the Captain and Admiral whilst the routine of the inspection is being settled and then the command 'Present the Officers.'

As our names are called out in the order of our seniority, we salute and step in front of our King who gives each a searching look, appraising and deciding, whilst he shakes hands as with a friend and shipmate. Our presentation over we stand on one side and watch the others as they come up, and even as we watch we catch another glimpse of the character of this sailorman. Simply, easily, and as of right he was taking over the command of the ship, and the other attributes of kingship were fading into the background. One could see it in the attitude of the Captain; he was no longer the senior officer but only the officer responsible to his captain; in the demeanour of the other officers and the lower deck ratings; near at hand there was the consciousness and acceptance of this same transformation. We were serving under our Captain, our Captain the King.

The youngest gunroom officer, blushing to the tips of his ears – there will be no need to censor his letters to-night for statements calculated to bring the Service into disrepute – but in no way embarrassed, has finished his handshake and the King turns to the Captain: 'Divisions, please.' And at the bugle call we melt away to our stations.

As the King approaches each company of seamen the officer in command gives the order 'Division! Shun! Off caps!' and each man is carefully and rapidly scrutinised. That part of the inspection over, the King proceeds to walk round the ship. Few questions are asked, there is no need for this man to have ships explained to him and any answers given are crisp and to the point.

I had gone to the big, light, airy Sick Bay (would it were behind armour!) and soon, from the tramping of feet and the bugle sounding the 'Still,' I know the King is approaching. As he enters the doorway I call my staff and invalids to attention, to have my order immediately cancelled by the King's 'Carry on!' For this man knows what it means to adopt a constrained attitude when sick, and will have none of it. He goes round the cots, asks just the right sailorman questions, speaks sympathetically to those who are in bed, and then turns to me to satisfy himself that all is well in my department.

'What are your fighting arrangements?'

I briefly answer this man who expects and needs no wordy explanations.

'Are they satisfactory? Have you any suggestions?' Then, casting a glance round the big compartment with its comfortable cots and shining equipment, 'They have improved these places since I first went to sea!'

I wondered what memories of the old *Bacchante* and *Thrush* these words were recalling.

Just as he turned to go he recollected something and turned to me again:

'Tell me. How did Taylor die? You know, he was a friend of mine.'

I knew the officer had been an old shipmate and I told how he had been killed during the Dogger action.

'He did not suffer at all?'

'No, Sir. He was killed outright.'

'I'm glad. You know there were rumours –'

I knew that shortly after the action a scoundrel who had left the ship had, for the sake of gain and the exaltation of his ego, written a lying account of the officer's last moments and that it had been published in one of the cheaply sensational weekly papers. But how did this man know?

'Absolutely impossible, Sir. I assure you he could have known nothing.'

The King thought for a moment, eyeing me gravely the while.

'Do you ever write to Mrs. Taylor?'

'I have done so, Sir.'

'If you write again tell her how sorry I am. I would have written myself but I have been so busy.'

And that evening as I passed forward through the mess decks to the Sick Bay I heard a Petty Officer discussing the inspection. In four words he gave the gist of the whole matter.

"'E knows, 'e does!'

* * *

Of course during this long period of apparent inaction, much was happening of interest to ourselves though not to a nation in arms against an almost overwhelming foe. As far as the Fleet was concerned all hopes of a decisive action at sea were rapidly disappearing. The initial German strategy of the war, namely to reduce the morale and numbers of the Grand Fleet by mine, submarine and isolated actions in which they were largely superior, had been a complete failure as far as reducing the disparity in numbers went. True, we had lost many vessels and men, but we could afford – dreadful word to use in such conjunction – these losses, as the ships were usually old and of little fighting value in a Fleet action. Powerful additions to the Grand Fleet, more than enough to compensate for our losses, were constantly arriving. The outlook looked like being a stalemate at sea just as it looked like being a stalemate on land.

During this period it struck somebody in authority that it would be as well if the Navy and Army had some idea about what each other was doing, and with the object of making them better acquainted, visits were interchanged, army officers spending a few days on board the ships and naval officers being sent to the trenches. Amongst those who were accommodated on board our ship was a Field officer. He was given a spare cabin near to mine and it fell to my lot to act as his sea daddy. He was a charming and interesting man and the decorations of his left breast had not been won in the snug security of Staff Headquarters. He expressed a hope that the Fleet might be ordered to sea during his stay.

The next morning after his arrival we were ordered to sea. It was blowing a full easterly gale as we passed under the Forth Bridge and steamed down the Firth through the submarine gates which had been opened for us. Further down the Firth and close to the Isle of May there was a really heavy sea which of course had no effect on our 33,000 tons displacement but which was hammering the escorting destroyers on our beam. Just before the Admiral signalled to the destroyers to return to port the soldier called my attention to one of them which, at 23 knots, had dived full tilt into a head sea. The whole of her forecastle and bows was completely hidden by an enormous wave which dashed aft until it met the structure of the bridge. It met this with a resounding whack and then leapt clean over the bridge, and we could see the remains of it falling down the forward funnel.

'Time for them to pack up!' I said.

'How do they live in it?' asked the soldier, pointing to the drenched crew huddled abaft any shelter they could find on her reeling deck.

'Wet, cold, hungry and frightened,' I said. 'The usual sailor's paradise.'

Once clear of the May Island we started zigzagging, and when we turned our beam to the seas the deck was no place for anyone with a leaning towards a dry skin, so we proceeded to the smoking room below. This was a luxurious apartment, of course, being a gun casemate with a six-inch gun in it, a settee and three or four Admiralty pattern armchairs, and a card table. A corticene covering to the steel deck and a few extra electric lights completed the equipment. The gun, of course, filled most of the compartment, and in racks round about were stowed the ready-for-use ammunition and the gun-cleaning implements. There was no daylight. In fine weather the doors closing the gun port would be swung outwards against the ship's side, but in bad weather or at night-time they were closed against the barrel of the gun, which was trained along the ship's side. The doors were not a very good fit and every time the sea hit the ship a squirt of water came through the chinks and joined its forerunners on the wet deck. In the centre of the casemate was the ammunition hoist, a devilish contraption about 2 feet high in the coamings with the lid held down and made watertight by the pressure of huge projecting butterfly nuts. There was no door, only a damp curtain, and our air, if the gods were kind and the ventilating system was working properly, was provided through a tube – as we called it 'tinned air.' This was our only retreat from the wardroom except our private cabins, and in action, during drill and at various other times the furniture was returned to the wardroom whence it came and the casemate closed to us.

The wardroom was close to the smoking room and was a long quadrilateral apartment running athwartships. It was almost completely filled by two long mahogany mess tables at which we took our meals, but there was also a small watch table at which the officers on watch took their meals, a stove with a couple of armchairs in front of it, and, in the after bulkhead, two cushioned lockers on which one could sit with a reasonable degree of comfort. The forward bulkhead had a buttery hatch opening into the combined pantry and galley. A door at either end of the room opened on to the alleyways. Daylight was admitted by a skylight opening on to the quarter-deck, but of course at sea in bad weather or when it was necessary to darken ship at night-time this was closed by steel hatch covers. In this compartment lived some thirty-three or thirty-four officers of wardroom rank. We could not all sit at table, but usually some officers were away at meal time, so we managed.

What Kipling calls our 'belly needs' were attended to by a Maltese messman. These Maltese messmen were supposed to be temporary service men, and the temporary character of their service usually lasted the whole of their lives. They brought with them their own cooks and wine stewards, and they beat their English confreres into a cocked hat. Ours was a jewel.

Breakfast was at 8 o'clock, lunch at 12, tea at 3.30, and dinner at 7 when at sea and at 7.30 in harbour. We did not dress for dinner during the War, our mess kit having been left on shore by Admiralty orders. We did wash, though, as dinner was the only formal meal of the day. A mess president was elected for the week, officers usually serving in rotation, and at dinner the Commander, who was the senior officer of the mess, sat at the president's right hand. The other officers sat where they chose, the vice-president occupying the chair opposite the president. Everyone tried to avoid sitting on the president's left, this position being known as starvation corner from the food being passed round so that this seat was served last. We were waited upon by our marine servants.

At dinner grace was always said by the chaplain. If he were not present the usual naval formula was always followed. Rapping with an ivory hammer on the table the president cast a glance round the table. 'No Padre here? Thank God!' After this the dinner was served and no officer could leave his seat before 'The King' without having received the permission of the president. Any infraction of the rules of the mess, such as mentioning a lady's name, was dealt with by the president fining the offender a glass of port all round the mess. We always sat at the toast of 'The King,' given by the president and answered by the vice with 'Gentlemen, The King', a jealously guarded privilege handed down from the days when an attempt at standing up was the prelude to a cracked crown against the beams overhead.

Of course there were other messes in the ship. The Captain, surely the loneliest man on God's sea, had his own domestic staff and lived in solitary state. The junior officers, such as sub-lieutenants and midshipmen, lived in the gunroom, presided over by the senior sub, who governed his unruly tribe with a rod of iron and dealt out his favourite punishment of one dozen with a dirk scabbard over the gunroom table. There was also the warrant officers' mess, presided over by the senior warrant officer – in our case the boatswain. Some day I hope someone will be able to tell the people of this Empire what they owe to the naval warrant officers. Promoted from the ranks, and officers in standing, their expert knowledge of life and duty both above and below decks is the backbone of an efficient ship.

Our wardroom officers were a motley crowd professionally. Besides the executive officers, of whom the Commander was the senior, there were engineer officers of all grades from a Captain downwards, two marine officers, a chaplain, a naval instructor for the benefit of the midshipmen, three medical officers, a Royal Naval Reserve lieutenant, three volunteer reserve lieutenants two of whom had been dragged from their school at Dartmouth College, and two paymasters. We sat together at meals in this small wardroom for over two years and got to know each other inside out and were usually on the best of terms with one another. We had our differences, of course, but they were merely ripples on the surface of the deep pool of our comradeship.

The soldier was deeply interested in our little kingdom. and seemed to be insatiable in his demands for information on points of dissimilarity between the two services. In spite of my warning about 'The King' I had to pull him down forcibly when he attempted to stand up, and he said afterwards he would have felt less self-conscious standing up when everybody else was sitting than he did sitting during the toast. Such is the compelling strength of ingrained habit.

The whole day had been rather dull and uninteresting, though the soldier was much impressed by his view of the big ships ploughing their way through the seas in the darkness, and about 10 o'clock he said he would like to turn in. I accompanied him down to his cabin to make sure everything was all right. His marine servant had just finished clearing up and was busy making ready for possible emergencies in the usual manner. Taking the high-backed chair he placed it with the back close up to the bunk within easy reach of the sleeper's arm, draped the swimming jacket over the back so that it could be picked up in an instant, and then with much puffing and blowing inflated the swimming collar and hung it on the back of the chair as well. After surveying his work with the eye of an expert, he nodded as one well satisfied and turned to the soldier.

'Anything else I can do for you, Sir?'

'Nothing, thank you.'

'Good-night, Sir."

'Good-night.'

The soldier was standing as if hypnotized, gazing fixedly at the back of his chair. Finally his eyes sought mine.

'Whatever in all the world is this for?'

'Just in case you have to swim for it,' I said. 'But for Heaven's sake don't put that collar on if you are going to jump from a height or you will break your blessed neck. Put it on after you get into the water, if your waistcoat isn't enough to float you.'

'But is this the usual routine?'

'Of course it is. Come into my cabin and you will see my gear all laid out just as yours is.'

He came into my cabin, and my chair seemed to exercise the fascination of a snake over him.

'But is this serious?' he asked, apparently doubtful whether he was being made the subject of a leg pull.

'Of course not,' was my answer. 'We'll probably never have a chance of using them if anything does happen.'

His expression was that of a man who has got into the wrong train and cannot find a porter to question.

'There's another thing,' I said. 'Come outside my cabin. Do you see that armoured door there? Well, should the alarm go during the night for Action Stations that door will automatically close, but very, very slowly. It takes about three minutes and before it is closed you must be on the other side of it; for once closed it stays closed, and although you can telephone up to the bridge and ask to have it reopened, it may not be possible to do so. This part of the ship where our cabins are is unarmoured and has already been damaged by enemy shell. On the other side of that door you are behind armour and as safe as we can make you.'

The soldier looked bewildered.

'Would you mind saying that again?' he asked.

'No, I won't,' I laughed. 'Don't you worry! If the alarm does go I'll come and dig you out in plenty of time.'

'Then perhaps I'd better sleep in my clothes.'

'No need! Just have them in a handy bundle ready to pick up and run if we do have to make a dash for it.'

The alarm did go about midnight and the soldier had the satisfaction of seeing an excited mob of hundreds of half-clad joking bluejackets melt into their fighting stations like magic. He had had to pick his bundle up and fly, but after finishing his toilet in one of the cabins behind armour he went over the ship and pronounced it good. It was only a drill and later we returned to bed.

Something had gone wrong with my supply of tinned air and after a few hours of unrefreshing sleep I woke up about five and struggled up to the quarter-deck. There I found the soldier in a similar half-baked condition to myself, and we moodily gazed over the wildly tumbling sea on which the early morning sun was sparkling. The ship was zig-zagging and little wisps of spoondrift were being blown across the quarter-deck so that we had to get under the lee of a turret.

Suddenly the soldier seized me by the arm and pointed excitedly to something in the sea ahead which a zig had just brought into view.

'Look! What in Heaven's name is that?'

I followed the direction of the pointing finger. Away on our port bow and looking as if we were actually heading for it was a round black object alternately rising and falling, appearing and disappearing in the sea. Even as I looked, it swung round and showed its horns.

'That,' I said sleepily, 'that's a German mine.'

'But we are heading straight for it. Does the bridge know? We're going to hit it!'

'Not a bit of it,' I assured him. 'That mine's adrift. I don't believe we could hit it if we tried. Our wash will keep it away from us. Only a moored mine is dangerous, and as for the bridge, what do you think that means?'

I nodded to where just abaft the battery a small group of marines were running out on the quarter-deck and, kneeling down, were bringing their rifles to the ready. The corporal gave the order and the men started taking pot shots at the mine in the hope of sinking it. It was rapidly left astern and whether it was hit and sunk as the marines claimed, I do not know.

I was more interested in the soldier. His face was working and he was muttering to himself.

'This is a horrible life! I shall thank God when I can get back to the trenches again.'

I roared with laughter. 'I always thank my lucky stars I have a ship to carry me into action, because I know perfectly well my flat feet would refuse to take me there.'

'Do you mean it?' he asked wonderingly.

New officers came to the mess and old officers went. I was rapidly becoming the oldest original inhabitant of the wardroom. Amongst those who went was our No. 2 gunnery officer, who was the son of a very distinguished physician, and perhaps for that reason there was a very strong bond of sympathy between us in spite of the marked disparity of our ages. In the evening after dinner it was his custom to come to my cabin where I sat reading or writing, draw aside the curtain – our doors were never shut; doors have been known to jam at awkward moments – hesitate for a moment whilst he asked if I were free, and then come in and yarn about everything under heaven. He was, as befitted his parentage, an exceptionally capable and clever officer, and clearly marked for rapid advancement in the Service. His one ambition was to be appointed to a ship as gunnery officer in charge.

One evening he came down to my cabin looking anxious and worried. In these nerve-wracking days not the least important of my duties was to keep a watchful eye on officers and men and on the least sign of overstrain to have them sent on leave, transferred to another quieter billet or discharged to a hospital ship. In reply to my question as to what was worrying him he told me he had just received his appointment as gunnery officer to a large cruiser lying at Invergordon. The appointment was a splendid one for an officer of his seniority, and I told him that he ought to consider himself lucky and congratulated him upon it. The only answer he would make was a constant reiteration of 'I don't want to go to that ship.' He loved the ship he was serving in, he adored the senior gunnery officer, who was one of the most brilliant men in the Service, he was happy with his present messmates, he had a dozen different reasons for his dislike for his new billet. It was easy to see that all this argument was only eyewash to conceal from himself his real reason for his unwillingness to join his new ship. At last I asked him plump and plain, 'What is your real reason?' Horribly distressed that he had been unable to justify his reluctance he blurted out, 'I tell you I don't know, I only know I don't want to go.'

Strictly speaking he should have taken up his appointment straight away, but he made as much delay as possible about turning over and remained for a day or two. At the end of that time we were ordered to sea and he was openly jubilant because for at least three or four days he need not leave. But on our return to Rosyth a telegram from his new Captain demanded that he should take up his appointment without any further delay. So he had to go, still showing every sign of unwillingness to leave.

Two nights afterwards as I lay asleep in my cabin it seemed to me that I was awake and sitting at my writing desk. I heard a footfall outside my cabin and then my curtain was pulled aside. Turning in my chair I saw my friend standing framed in the doorway but looking not at me but far beyond me. In my dream I too looked at him and beyond him, seeing unutterable things. Then I spoke softly, 'But you are dead, you know.' He nodded slightly and seemed to answer, 'Yes, I know.' Even as I looked I heard the rattle of the rings as the curtain was pulled back into position again. I woke up in my dark cabin shivering, and through the curtain could see the glimmer of the electric lights in the flats outside.

Next day we heard that his ship had been blown up in Invergordon harbour and practically everybody on board had been killed. He had been barely twenty-four hours aboard her.

During this period we heard much about spies, and although there were probably plenty of them watching us we had very little experience of their activities except on one occasion. A young lieutenant was joining the ship from one of the barracks and had to catch his train from King's Cross. He was very much all right inside but his outside was not particularly attractive to the wandering female eye and in consequence of this he was almost the only man in uniform on the platform who was not being seen off by a bevy of home comforts. One can imagine his surprise and appreciation when a very beautiful young lady detached herself from a group, came up to him quite openly and frankly, said she was sorry to see he was all alone and asked whether he was going to join his ship. He said that he was, and the girl told him that she did not know any sailors although she knew plenty of soldiers, and she chatted pleasantly about his life on board and how dull they must find it cut off from so much that made the lot of the soldier so interesting and amusing whilst on duty in England. The whole interview was delightful and on hearing that the officer had no girl correspondents she offered to supply the deficiency. At that time the 'lonely soldier' correspondence stunt was all the rage, and so far nothing had happened that was, from the war point of view, unusual.

The correspondence thus initiated was continued for some months. In her letters were frequent questions on many subjects to which a reply was forbidden, but the officer put this down to the girl's confessed ignorance of all naval affairs. But the last letter received from her contained the suggestion that if he could let her know where the ship was likely to be on a certain date the writer would make an effort to come and see him. This letter rather worried him. He was desperately keen on seeing the girl again but he was doubtful whether he should give the information necessary to bring about the happy event. In his dilemma he brought the letter to me, as any answer would have to pass through my hands as censor.

We discussed the question for a long time. The officer had no illusions as to his appearance and he agreed that it was not likely, 'though women being funny things you could never be quite sure,' that a beauty such as he described would be likely to endure the long journey up to Scotland just for the sake of a second view of his ugly mug and that it might be a trap. I suggested referring the matter to the Captain, and if he approved the necessary information could be sent. The Captain took a serious view of the affair, probably because he knew how much the date mattered, and suggested referring the letter to our Intelligence Department in order to establish the bona fides of the lady.

The only news we ever had of the result was when the Intelligence people thanked the officer for supplying them with the address of a nest of spies whom they had been trying to round up for a long time.

Chapter VIII
The North Sea

If any attempt be made to understand the chief occupation of the British Fleet in war-time, it is first of all necessary to have an intelligent comprehension of the physical geography of that patch of water separating the eastern coasts of Great Britain from the Continent of Europe, and known as the North Sea. In our older school maps it was also marked 'or German Ocean,' but the claim to the latter title has lapsed since August 4, 1914, and will not be revived, in all probability, during the lifetime of any of us.

This North Sea has peculiar characteristics, many of them exceptionally favourable to the operations of the German Fleet, and few of them favourable to the British. Our ships were built to serve in any climate and against any enemy, whilst the Germans built theirs with the prime object of threatening the British coasts and only operating in the North Sea, within a few hundred miles of their bases. Just as it is true that the specialist in all professions must be more competent in his specialised subjects than his more catholic brethren, so the specialised German Fleet in this area undoubtedly possessed certain advantages over the generalised British Fleet. This superiority was confined to his ships and methods of warfare and their adaptation to the particular duties they were designed for.

It is hoped in this description of the North Sea to clear up these points, so that the non-seagoing reader may grasp just what these advantages are and how they imposed certain dispositions on the British Fleet, and also how this superiority was met and overcome by the British seamen and their Allies.

If we take a line from Unst in the Shetland Islands to Bergen in Norway, and two other lines – one from Unst and the other from The Naze – to the Channel at Dover, we are enclosing a roughly triangular space which, for purposes of the present warfare, may be described as the North Sea. The only entrances to this area from the Atlantic are through the Straits of Dover, by way of the English Channel, or across the line Unst-Bergen. Passage through the Straits of Dover can be readily barred by mechanical means, but the line Unst-Bergen is 180 miles long (a channel 3 miles wide along its eastern border is the territorial waters of Norway), and can only be closed by patrolling cruisers. There are also two narrow passages between the Shetlands and Orkneys and between the Orkneys and the North of Scotland, but, like the Dover Straits, they can easily be closed to hostile traffic. For all practical purposes, it may be asserted that when Germany was blockaded by the British Fleet, exit from the North Sea was only possible to her across the line Unst-Naze. The line Unst-Bergen can easily be blockaded by the British Fleet up to a point, so that exit by the northern route is almost impossible. But, unfortunately, there is such a thing as the 3-mile limit, and any enemy ship which cares to do so can pass up the North Sea within the neutral waters of Norway and, though she may be plainly visible to the blockading fleet, they have no power to bring her to action.

It was impolitic to blockade the coast of Norway – who would have objected to such a procedure just as much as the United States did. As the blockading fleet could not possibly pretend to watch the whole of the coast of Norway, there was nothing to prevent a mercantile or fighting submarine passing up the coasts of Norway to any point she pleased, and from there dashing across the Atlantic to the United States. When travelling on the surface, no submarine would be visible at a distance of over 4 miles, whilst her antagonist could be picked up at perhaps as much as 10 miles, thus giving the submarine time to submerge until such time as she thought it safe to emerge. As there is nothing in ordinary weather to give any indication of the direction in which the submarine is travelling under water, the surface ship is entirely at a loss as to what direction she must travel in. The surface ship also dare not remain at rest near where the submarine submerged, as, if it were a fighting ship, it might have the opportunity of sinking the surface vessel. So as she moves on she may be making a course diametrically opposed to that of the submarine.

There was nothing wonderful about the mercantile submarines managing to evade the blockade, but it is marvellous that in spite of their handicap the British patrolling fleet should have succeeded in bringing the career of some of these same submarines to an untimely end.

Studying the chart of the North Sea, its shallowness is the first characteristic impressed upon one. Except for a curious deep-water channel of about 150 fathoms depth and 50 miles width, running along the west coast of Norway, southward round the Naze and up into the Skager Rock, there is no place in the whole area where the depth is over 90 fathoms. Starting at the line Unst-Bergen, the depth is 65 to 85 fathoms, and working southward the depth gradually and uniformly decreases, until 20 miles off Heligoland it is only 20 fathoms, and the same distance off the coasts of Holland and Belgium it is about 15 fathoms. From these distances the coast gradually shelves shoreward, so that the 10-fathom line runs down the coast on an average about 12 miles from it. Off the coast of England are numberless sandbanks and shallow patches, and these considerably restrict the navigable area; and the same kind of obstruction encumbers, in a bewildering manner, the coasts of Germany, Holland and Belgium. The largest of these sandbanks is the well-known Dogger Bank, and this has a big patch with only 7 to 9 fathoms of water on it, lying about 65 miles from Spurn Head. There are numerous other banks running parallel to the English coast, and all of them dangerous to large ships. As most of the buoys and lightships marking these dangers were removed when the War started, and celestial observations, which are the only safe method of finding the position of the ship, were often impossible for days together, it is needless to point out the difficulties that beset the navigator.

Tides run strongly and uncertainly, so that positions calculated by dead reckoning alone are often untrustworthy; thus when a ship reports that she is engaged with the enemy in such and such a position, the point arrived at by the supporting ships may be separated from the point desired by 10, 15 or even 20 miles.

The distances across the North Sea are short. From the Forth to Jutland is only about 400 miles, and from the Humber to Heligoland about 240. These short distances must be remembered when we come to speak of the relative speeds of the two fleets.

It is obvious that an enemy ship doing 25 knots can cross from Heligoland to the Humber in ten hours, and that if she is pursued by a 26-knot ship from the mouth of the Humber, a 10-mile start will mean that the German ship will be under the protection of the land forts before the British vessel can bring her to action.

As the British were always the pursuing vessels, the enemy had the advantage of being able to direct the action into any waters they chose, and then generally tried to bring the British into a previously mined area, in which they knew the channels, or signalled to their submarines to lie in wait at such and such a point. This manoeuvre was carried out successfully in the Dogger Bank action, which had to be broken off by Beatty on account of the presence of enemy submarines, and again in the affair in the North Sea in September 1916, when the *Falmouth* and *Nottingham* were sunk.

Except for an hour or so during the battle of Jutland, when the Germans thought they had the British Battle Cruiser Fleet only to deal with, they always attempted to avoid an action. When the British bluejacket moaned that the German Fleet would not come out, he did not mean that they never put to sea. What he meant was that they always avoided a fight, unless they thought that the enemy would be foolish enough to follow them across previously prepared mine and submarine areas. The object of the 'tip and run' expeditions was to get public opinion to force the Commander-in-Chief's hands, so that in a future raid he would order our ships to chase and engage the enemy at all costs. What annoyed the British bluejacket more than anything else was that the German always acted on the presumption that our officers were idiots and utterly incompetent. Treading on the tail of your enemy's coat is a poor game, unless you know what the coat covers.

The weather in the North Sea is usually bad. According to statistics published in the *North Sea Pilot*, the wind has been found to blow with a force of five or over on an average of ten days during every month throughout the year, and with a force of ten or over twice every month during October to March. A force of five or over means a full summer gale, while a force of ten or over means a hurricane. During the summer, from April to September, on eight days of the month, visibility is only 4,000 yards; on eight days 8,000 yards; and on the remaining days over 8,000 yards. Obviously, fog or mist is to be expected on more than half the days in summer, and in winter the conditions of visibility are only very slightly better. To emphasise what this means, it should be stated that the actions of Jutland and the Dogger Bank commenced at ranges of 18,000 to 21,000 yards.

From the official statements quoted above, it can be gathered that if the British Fleet proceeded to sea for three days, on one of the days they would meet a gale which might rise to the force of a hurricane, one of the days would be foggy or so misty that gunnery would be difficult, and one of the days would probably be good fighting weather. If the Fleet desired to avoid action, it could count on doing so for two days of the three it remained at sea. This was of immense advantage to the Germans, allowing them to decide nearly always whether they would fight or not.

Of course these figures and statistics are all based upon averages. It is possible, and quite frequent, in winter to go to sea for three days and meet nothing but gales, to have nothing except fog and mist for three days in summer, and to have three days of perfect weather for enemy-hunting in spring or autumn. And, alas! it happened, with fortunate results for the German Fleet, that often there were days when the weather can best be described as samples.

The waves thrown up by gales in the North Sea are those peculiar to shallow waters. They are short, curling, breaking hillocks of yellowish-green sea, exceedingly trying to small vessels, which pitch and tumble and roll, and, if pressed against it, would rapidly strain and seriously injure themselves. It was a wonderful sight to see them steaming straight into it, their bows diving into the breaker as it curled over and buried the whole of the forecastle, whilst the spray flew in huge masses right over their mastheads. On account of the danger to life and structure they were nearly always obliged to proceed at reduced speed when steaming against even a summer gale. The big ships, of course, could crash through it to their heart's content, but the motion was exceedingly violent at times, making accurate gunnery almost impossible, and they looked like half-tide rocks when the short seas they failed to rise to broke over them. It takes a chapter all to itself to depict as faithfully as is possible the sensations of being driven into a heavy sea, and they need not be dilated upon here.

The instruments of destruction employed in naval warfare are the mine, the torpedo and the gun. The chief weapon depended upon by the British was the gun, although they used the torpedo to a fair extent and the mine very little. The chief weapons employed by the Germans were the mine and the torpedo. The gun was only used by them to a slight extent, and then unsuccessfully, except in the battle of Coronel.

Except in the early days of the war, the torpedo only scored legitimately against the *Falmouth* and the *Nottingham*, and the remainder of the German successes against our ships in the North Sea were by means of the mine. The torpedo was relegated by the Germans to the position of the chief weapon against harmless merchant ships.

Without entering into detail, it may be accepted as beyond dispute that the ideal conditions for successful mine-laying are supplied by navigable channels amongst sandbanks. The sandbanks restrict the area in which the mine-field need be laid, and in the channel the mines can be laid rapidly, keep automatically at their depth of 14 feet much better, and have many more chances of intercepting their unsuspecting victims. The mines must be moored, of course, so that they may not drift into positions in which they would be harmless, or possibly as dangerous to the layers as to their enemies. It is a regulation of the Hague Convention that a mine should at once become harmless if it gets adrift from its moorings; but this is not always easy to arrange, and whether from malice or mechanical difficulties, the German mines always signally failed to comply with this regulation.

In certain cases the German deliberately violated the Hague Convention by throwing overboard floating mines when pursued by our ships, and the loss at least of one of our submarines and probably many merchant ships, was due to this cause in one of the Yarmouth raids. Counting, as usual, on the Britisher being an utter fool, he also sowed floating mines in certain places on the high seas, which showed an attachment above the water, closely resembling the periscope of a submarine. Evidently he thought that the British would ram these mines and be blown up; but the officer of a ship who would do such a thing without seeing the feather which invariably accompanies a real submarine is unknown in the British Navy, and this ruse was a complete failure, as far as men-of-war were concerned. There can be no reasonable doubt, however, that merchant ships stumbled in the dark on these periscope mines and were blown up.

Remembering the description of the configuration of the bottom of the North Sea, it will be readily understood that it was easy for the Germans to mine their own short length of coast, leaving only navigable channels which could be constantly changed by sweeping and remining for the use of their battleships when they went to sea. For the British to mine protectively their own 600 miles of eastern coast was practically impossible, not to mention the large element of danger to the enormous volume of coastwise traffic which such a procedure would have involved. But for the Germans to mine offensively our coasts without regard to the laws of humanity or war was comparatively easy, and when done by submarines it was almost impossible of detection, except by sweeping or the blowing up of a ship. As long as the German mine was moored it was liable to be hit by a ship, but as soon as it was adrift the high speed at which our fighting ships usually travelled washed them along the side of the vessel, and they nearly always failed to explode. The slow-moving merchant ship does not cause the same amount of wash, and many of them fell victims to the German mine far away from the place where it was originally laid.

Early in the War, most of the German minefields off our coasts were laid by above-water vessels, but it is pretty safe to say that none of them were laid in this manner after 1916, this work being done thereafter entirely by specially fitted submarine vessels, one of which was captured and exhibited in the Thames. The procedure of dropping mines is always referred to in His Majesty's Navy as 'laying eggs,' and when a ship explodes one she is said to have 'hatched it.'

The mine is a purely passive agent of destruction, and requires that the ship should come to it and should be unsuspecting. As mines are usually moored at a depth of 14 feet below the surface, so that their presence may not be readily detected by the rise and fall of the waves in rough weather, it follows that they are only dangerous to large vessels of deep draught. The mine-sweepers and small coasting craft paid not the slightest heed to the presence of a mine-field, and steamed merrily about in areas where larger ships would have met with certain destruction.

From the description given it will be readily understood that the mine is a very uncertain instrument of warfare, and when one considers the losses caused to the British Navy by mines laid by Germans, it is exceedingly doubtful whether they justified the enormous expenditure incurred by their use. They require to be laid in overwhelming numbers; the ships employed are very expensive, as they have to be large, fast and elaborately fitted. In one case, at any rate, the *Yorck*, and probably in many other instances of which we heard rumours but no definite information, the miner was hoisted by his own petard.

The first naval action of the War was the sinking of a German mine-layer by one of His Majesty's light cruisers. Many mine-fields were also laid without causing injury to a single British fighting ship.

From the actively hostile point of view, the German mine was a failure. But the knowledge of its possible or probable existence has a powerful moral effect on the commanding officers of fleets. No admiral would dare to court disaster by leading his fleet over a known mined area, so that for defensive purposes along a short stretch of coastline, such as the navigable approaches to Germany, in the North Sea, the mine is a cheap and certain weapon. Even though it should not be there, the probability that a certain area is mined will keep the hostile fleet away.

The only method of attacking a mined coast is by first sweeping a channel, but this is an exceedingly slow process. It requires that the trawlers should be well backed up by strong forces, and renders the supporting ships an easy prey to submarine attack. Against a determined enemy, it would almost certainly result in heavy losses of ships.

The torpedo is the weapon *par excellence* of the submarine and the destroyer. The destroyer, of course, is an above-water craft, and its movements are plain to be seen and countered by other destroyers, the more powerful light cruisers, and battle cruisers. But the submarine is on another footing altogether. Invisibility to the enemy is its chief asset, but as its under-water speed is low – rarely over 14 knots – it cannot chase the above-water ships. Its best chance of striking a blow, therefore, is to lie about somewhere near the entrance to harbours or frequented channels and trust more or less to chance that luck will bring a ship near enough for it to fire a torpedo with every probability of hitting. Should it fire and miss, it will have betrayed its presence, and must at once submerge to a depth of at least 40 feet to avoid the zig-zag rushes of the enemy. As it must show its periscope on coming to the surface, the probability is that it will be seen before it can see, and find the forefoot of a destroyer in unpleasant proximity to its hull. Therefore, having fired its shot, the submarine usually at once makes for the bottom and remains there, or steers blindfold a course deep down, which it hopes will take it away from the dangerous area. Every submarine officer knows when he has fired a shot, whether successful or not, that the next time he emerges may be his last moment on earth. The courage of some of our submarine officers can be gauged from the fact that, despite the risks, some of them fired two shots at enemy ships at very short intervals.

I have said that the submarine must submerge to a depth of 40 feet below the water level, so as to avoid the keels of the warships, many of which draw well over 30 feet. The body of the submarine is probably about 20 feet in diameter, so that to be able to manoeuvre at that depth there must be at least 13 or 14 fathoms of water where they are working. Greater depths than these are usual in the main navigable channels to all the principal British naval ports in the North Sea, but as has been already remarked, this depth can only be found 10 to 15 miles out from the channels to the German ports. To keep up an efficient blockade at this distance out would require a submarine at least every 5 miles for the 180 miles stretch, meaning, with reliefs and allowances for passages, probably well over a hundred submarines. Even if it were possible to supply this number and to keep them in their proper stations – a matter of extreme difficulty amongst the strong tides and patches of outlying shallow water – the very multiplication of numbers would ensure a steady supply of victims to the enemy anti-submarine tactics.

In spite of the very real advantages conferred upon them by our narrow deep-water channels, the German submarines only torpedoed three ships in the North Sea during eighteen months. It is not surprising that our own submarines, confronted with much greater difficulties, were not much more successful. Our ships constantly patrolled the North Sea, whilst the larger ships of the German fleet rarely emerged from the shelter of their mine-fields. When the weather was stormy in the shallow southern waters, our submarines were subjected to the motion called 'pumping,' which can best be likened to the up-and-down motion in the water which can be imparted to an almost sinking body by pushing it downwards. This rising and falling in rapid succession may be for as much as 30 feet, and is exceedingly trying to the crews. Such pumping motion can be avoided off our coasts by submerging in depths of over 20 fathoms.

The torpedo – usually known as a 'fish' or 'mouldy' in the service – is practically a self-propelled mine, the machinery of which is driven by compressed air. It is fired by compressed air or powder from a torpedo-tube, the object of the firing merely being to get it clear of the ship's side and start it on its initial course. By an elaborate system of horizontal and vertical rudders, controlled by a gyroscope, it returns to its original course when temporarily deflected, and maintains its position at a depth of about 12 to 15 feet. At the forward end is the live head, filled usually with a charge of tri-nitro-toluene, and on the head striking an object, a percussion arrangement detonates the explosive. The depth it runs at is calculated, so that it can reach the unprotected vitals of the enemy. It is comparatively slow, the speed of many of our fast fighting ships closely approaching it. It is fairly easily turned aside from its course by waves or the wash of a ship, but after swinging about for a little the gyroscope pulls it back again. It has a range of anything up to 10 miles, but is rarely used at this distance. Its greatest successes, as in the early days of the War in the North Sea and the Dardanelles, were when it was fired at point-blank range.

If a hole a foot square be made in the bottom of a ship at a point 9 feet below the water line, the water will enter at the rate of 2,470 tons per hour, and if it be 13 feet square, which would not be a large hole to be caused by the explosion of a torpedo, the water will enter at the rate of over 30,000 tons an hour. There are no pumps made on board a ship which could cope with a thirtieth part of this inrush, so that the safety of the ship must depend on the number of her water-tight compartments and the strength of her bulkheads. The older ships were not so minutely subdivided and strengthened as the more modern ones, which accounts for the fact that the ships torpedoed early in the war sank very quickly, whilst the *Marlborough* seven minutes after being struck was again taking her place in the fighting line.

Throughout the War the British public never quite realised the important part in the fighting that visibility takes. In all the reports of actions visibility was referred to again and again; but it must be insisted upon that visibility is not of so much importance in the matter of seeing clearly as seeing at a distance. All ships are compromises between weight and speed. It is impossible to combine both. You can have heavy armour, heavy guns, huge coal capacity, and therefore long-distance steaming powers and low speed; or light guns, light armour, small fuel capacity, and high speed, or any combination of the two conditions you please. British men-of-war are built to fight in any part of the world, and therefore heavy guns, light armour, and large fuel capacity with moderate speed have been considered the more advantageous combination. The German ships were built to fight in the North Sea, and the North Sea only, and they decided upon light guns, heavy armour, low fuel capacity, and moderate speed, compared with our ships of the same class. At long ranges, the advantage of the heavier guns more than counterbalances the protection of the heavier armour. At short ranges, the smaller gun has penetrating power against thin armour probably equal to our heavier guns against the thicker armour. In the North Sea the greater fuel capacity of the British ships is of little value.

In a previous paragraph it was stated that on sixteen days out of thirty the visibility in the North Sea was under 8,000 yards. That means, of course, that in action on sixteen days out of thirty, the British fleet lost the well-marked advantage to be derived from fighting at long ranges. The Germans counted upon this, and hence their relative proportions of guns and armour.

Class for class, the smaller guns of the German Fleet would probably pierce the thinner armour of the British ships, whilst their heavier armour would protect them better against our heavier armament. Of course when our big guns did pierce, the explosion was much more destructive than the shells of small calibre of the enemy; but direct hits with big guns are not frequent occurrences.

The German gunners apparently could not stand punishment as well as the British. When the ranges closed their heavy gun-firing became wild and made few hits. As they carried a large number of guns in their secondary armament, it was not surprising that in the tornado of firing a few of these latter should occasionally find a target. On the other hand, the British gunnery steadily improved as the action progressed, and at fairly close ranges the hitting by our big guns was most marvellously rapid and accurate, and in the battle of Jutland finally did so much damage that the Germans broke off the engagement and fled.

The difficulties in the way of hitting the target in sea fighting are very numerous. Compared with land artillery, the following are the more important: Neither the gun platform nor the target is fixed, as both are moving through the water at speeds which are not uniform. Besides the forward movement the range is constantly closing and opening, and as the result of a slight alteration in course, a change of only 90 feet will make all the difference between a hit and a miss at long ranges. The gun platform, i.e. the ship itself, is unsteady either from the movement of the sea or the motion imparted to the ship by the recoil of the guns. Should the shell not fall exactly on the required position in land fighting, it may still do a great deal of damage. At sea a miss is as good as a mile, although in the battle of the Dogger Bank the *Kolberg* is said to have been sunk by overs from H.M.S. *Tiger*.

The first principle of strategy in naval warfare is the same as strategy on land, and is directed towards engaging the enemy with superior forces. If a fleet is split up into small squadrons, the enemy has nothing to do but bring out all his fleet in force and destroy these squadrons *seriatim* before the others can come up in support. The British superiority in numbers was not great enough, and never could be great enough, to allow us to keep isolated squadrons scattered all over the coast in order to protect it from raids. I have already stated the reasons why the German coast can be easily rendered immune from raids and why ours is so vulnerable. When the enemy made a raid on our coasts, what he always hoped is that the panic caused by these raids might force the Admiralty to split up our Fleet, so that it would be employed purely in local defence. Should that policy ever be adopted, the end of the British supremacy at sea is within sight. The Germans need only send a few ships across to keep the isolated squadrons busy while the main fleet attacks and destroys the depleted Grand Fleet. They thought they had managed just such a manoeuvre at the battle of Jutland – that the Battle Cruiser Fleet was isolated from the Grand Fleet, and that they had nothing to do but devour the units at their leisure. Probably they have a little more respect for the British strategy now. Later on in the War, by impressing the British public by futile Channel raids, they hoped to raise such an outcry as would compel the Admiralty to adopt a dangerous policy. Unfortunately, a part of our Press invariably plays into the enemy's hands, and this time it did its best to force the Admiralty to do what was criminally wrong by asking, in a headline, 'Who rules the North Sea?'

If only the questioner had been on board one of those raiding German vessels he would soon have been supplied with the only possible answer: 'The British Navy rules the North Sea.'

Chapter IX
Jutland

The time is seven bells in the afternoon watch, and in the wardroom of one of His Majesty's battle cruisers a yawning marine servant with tousled hair and not too conspicuously clean a face is clattering cups and saucers at regular intervals round the two long tables which are the most obvious objects to be seen. Although it is a bright summer's day on deck, the electric lights are lit, the wardroom skylights are battened down, and the heavy bomb-proof shutters pulled into position. In all the ship, fore and aft, there is not a space where normal daylight can enter except in a few of the senior officers' cabins and down the companion-ways. Without being actually dirty, the whole living spaces are dingy and depressing. On the mess decks the watch below are indulging in their afternoon 'caulk,' stretched out on the tables or stools, with their heads resting on their wooden ditty boxes, which are used as pillows. Their forms are covered by watch coats, old hammocks, or pieces of deck cloth, for the wind blows chilly in the North Sea even on the thirty-first of May.

The wardroom is as depressing as the men's quarters. It measures roughly 30 feet by 20 feet; the walls are of white painted steel; the floor is of steel covered with corticine, which has been coated with red shellac varnish so that it may not absorb moisture. There are two doorways opening on the port and starboard sides. The furniture is of the simplest possible description, consisting of the two long tables already mentioned, a smaller table, two sofas, three easy-chairs, two fixed settees about 10 feet long, a dilapidated-looking piano covered with bundles of torn music, and two sideboards in alcoves, in each of which is a sliding hatch communicating with the pantry. The walls are bare except for a photograph of the sinking *Blücher*, an engraving of an earlier namesake of the ship, and some charts and war maps, hanging limply from drawing-pins, which fix them to wooden battens. In one corner is a coal stove, the polished brass funnel of which, passing to the deck above, is the only bright object in the room. Suspended from the beams by their cords and covered with yellow silken shades whose colour has long ago lost its pristine freshness and daintiness, are the electric lights. The gentle swaying of the shades is the only indication that the ship is at sea. Thanks to her turbine machinery, no noise or movement can be felt, and she might be lying in harbour for all there is to indicate otherwise.

The ship herself is one of the mammoths of the sea. When describing her in comparison with any other ship, apply superlatives and you will dimly reach some idea of her qualities. She is the largest, fastest, most heavily armed, best armoured, best equipped, highest horse-powered, best arranged engine of destruction of her time. Compared with a merchant ship, she has over twice the horsepower of the *Aquitania*. Her crew is well over a thousand. She has been blooded already, and her officers have supreme confidence in her and themselves. For over an hour, practically single-handed, she has fought the fleeing German battle cruisers, whilst her supporting consorts were endeavouring to catch her up.

A huge teapot containing a gallon of so-called tea is dropped with a thud on one of the wardroom sideboards. Plates are rattled violently as they are served around the table; there is a crash from the pantry as the third-class officers' steward, who has been sleeping on top of the sink, strikes his yawning elbow against a pile of dirty tumblers left over since lunch-time, and the marine servant shouts out: 'Tea is ready, gentlemen, please!'

There is a general movement from the settees, sofas and armchairs where tired officers have been snatching a brief rest. Four uncurl themselves from the small table where they have been sitting on high-backed chairs with their heads resting upon their arms. There is a general movement towards the long tables where the cups, saucers and plates show up startlingly white against the approved Admiralty pattern of serge tablecloth, whose main recommendation to the chooser must have been that it did not show the dirt. The dark red flowers have long ago become hopelessly mixed with the black background which is its most prominent feature when new.

The officers – there are thirty when they are all mustered – sit down at the tables and stare in front of them with the glassy, fixed eyes and owlish expression of those newly awakened from unrefreshing slumber in a tainted atmosphere. The marine servant, helped by another, carries round the enormous tin teapot and carelessly splashes a portion of the fluid into each cup as he passes. On the table are jugs containing 'tinned cow' and basins of brown sugar which the officers push to one another. For food there is good bread, butter and jam, and some musty fragments of old cake. For five minutes or so the meal is consumed in silence, when a signal messenger enters the wardroom and, with an air of conscious importance, lays a signal on the table beside the senior officer present. That individual gazes casually at it for a second, and then is suddenly galvanised into action. Holding it in both hands, he reads out eagerly: 'Flag to all ships. Our light cruisers report that they have just sighted an enemy light cruiser.'

There is silence for a moment and then a voice is heard: 'So much the worse for the enemy light cruiser!'

The scraping of the chairs against the floor is heard as they are hastily pushed back and the occupants rise, looking for their caps. No need to tell them what that signal means. 'Action stations' will be sounded in a few minutes.

A few whose duties are not so urgent remain behind, making hasty efforts at finishing their tea. They guess it will be a long time before they get a chance of another meal.

'I'm a conscientious objector,' says an engineer officer. 'I want to go home to mummy.'

'And I'm a pacifist,' remarks a lieutenant, 'but that's no reason why I should drink filth as well as think it. Waiter! bring me a cup of freshly-made tea, and don't let the dog get this or you'll poison him.'

One little cruiser from the Spiritual Home
Met the British battle boats – and then there were none!

sang in unmelodious, raucous tones a paymaster.

'Oh, shut up!' said another. 'There it goes.'

The bugle-call for 'Action stations' was heard, gradually getting louder as the bugle-boy ran along the passage outside.

'That puts the hat on it! No tea, no nuffink! Now for a drop of frightfulness. Wonder whether Fritz has any new gas shells.'

'Put your respirator on first and sniff afterwards,' said a doctor, as they crushed through the doorway together. 'If you really want to sell that Gieve you were blowing about yesterday, I'll give you an I.O.U. for a bob for it.'

'No good!' replied the lieutenant. 'I've sold it to a snotty for a quid. His people sent him two pounds ten to buy one, and we went a burst on the thirty bob.'

'Well, so long!' said the doctor, as they parted at the bottom of a ladder. 'If you fall into my hands you will be more cut up than I shall be.'

'Go to the devil, you bloodthirsty abomination,' shouted the lieutenant, and, seizing the rungs, ran rapidly up the horizontal ladder.

As he reached the upper deck and ran along towards the bridge ladders, he cast a glance round the horizon. 'Visibility so-so!' he thought; 'but if it gets no worse than at present it will do. Can see 18,000 easily. Clouds a bit low though – not much more than a thousand up.'

He ran up the bridge ladders and finally reached the upper bridge, where the captain and navigating officer, officer of the watch, and signalmen were busy getting ready to go down to the armoured conning-tower. Above him towered the foremast, a central thick steel tube supported by two smaller steel tubes running down and outwards to the deck. On the after side of the central tube, dropped steel rungs were let into the mast; and, seizing hold of these, he climbed rapidly upwards until he reached the trap-door communicating with the top. Pushing up the door, he pulled himself bodily upwards and at last stood on the platform, 120 feet above the level of the sea.

He was in a circular box about 10 feet in diameter, covered with a roof and with bulwarks rising breast-high all the way round. His duty was spotting for the secondary armament, and to assist him there were two other officers and eight men acting as range-takers, messengers, timekeepers, and in charge of deflection instruments. He gave the range for the guns to the transmitting station, watched the fall of the shot, estimated its distance over or short of the target, and supplied the necessary corrections. As it was useless to expect that firing the secondary guns would be of any value until the range came down to about 12,000 yards, or to repel destroyer or light cruiser attack, there would be a long interval of waiting before he would have anything to do. Meanwhile, he went round the instruments and saw that they were all in working order, tested the voice-tubes, and gave hints and instructions to his subordinates.

The sky was rapidly becoming more overcast and the clouds were lower, although the horizon was still plainly visible.

A message came up the voice-tube from the conning-tower, warning him to keep a sharp lookout on the port bow as the enemy battle cruisers should be shortly sighted proceeding in a northerly direction. Every sense was subordinated to that of sight, and in the tense stillness he strained his eyes until the sockets hurt. Looking down on the ship, which was spread like a map beneath his feet, no sign of life was visible, although behind armoured side and beneath thick steel hoods eager-eyed men were chafing at the delay.

It was easy to see that the ships were travelling at full speed, and the smoke belching from the ships ahead blurred his view and damaged his eyes until he remembered the pair of motor goggles he had supplied himself with.

Suddenly his attention was riveted by a small patch of the horizon where the haze seemed slightly thicker than elsewhere. To anyone who had not spent long weary hours watching for just such a haze it would have suggested nothing at all, even if it had been observed. He picked up his binoculars, which were hanging round his neck from a strap, and took a long, long look.

The other two officers watched his face carefully. Suddenly he dropped the glasses from his eyes and turned to his companions. 'Yes; that's the enemy battle cruisers all right. They are making a sixteen-point turn. I wonder what their game is. Are they running away as they did at the Dogger Bank, or are they falling back on the High Seas Fleet. Anyhow, there's the *Engadine* sending up a seaplane.'

He watched the movements of the seaplane ship for a few minutes, and then heaved a sigh of relief as a gigantic bird rose in flight from her side.

'We haven't sighted any of their Zeppelins yet and they would be useless in this atmosphere. If I know anything of the *Engadine*'s people we shall get all the information we need in a little.'

If anything, there was an access of speed on the part of the British ships. The officers in the top cowered behind the steel bulwark which protected them a little; but tiny hurricanes played around their coats and caps and pierced the almost Arctic clothing they were wearing.

The enemy ships were rapidly becoming distinguishable as funnels and masts hurrying beneath a pall of smoke. The hulls were still under the rim of the horizon, but were gradually rising.

'When we can see the hulls the range will be approximately 24,000 yards, and firing will open any time after that,' remarked the lieutenant to an officer whose first action this was.

Meanwhile, the range-finder was being rapidly adjusted by an able seaman who, seated behind it, commenced singing out in a monotonous voice with the suspicion of a shake of excitement in it: '22,000 – 20,500 – 19,000 – 18,000.'

As he reached the last figure, there was a spattering sound in the seas on their port side, and huge columns of spray were thrown 200 feet up in the air. Driven back by the wind, sheets of water swept against the top and drenched the luckless crew. Heedless, the lieutenant watched the fall of the shot and muttered: 'Five hundred short. Damned good effort at opening the ball.'

As he spoke there was a thundering roar from the ship beneath him, and he instinctively stepped back from the edge of the top to avoid the blast from the gun. 'That's "A" turret firing'; and as he traced the flight of the huge projectile which was plainly visible winging its way towards the distant speck, he waited anxiously for the splash which would indicate its fall. 'Good hunting! About five hundred short, too!'

These were not his guns and were not under his control; but he knew that the capable lieutenant spotting in the gun control tower below him, and the warrant officer in the top 20 feet above him, would speedily correct the error. His job was to wait and watch.

The action had become general. Shells, looking like Gargantuan hailstones, were falling on every side of him, while columns of water, like geysers, were rising everywhere and obscuring the range. As a shell whizzed past them and its breath pushed them farther back into the top, a shout of admiration escaped him. 'Straddled in the third salvo! Oh, by Jove! good shooting! Hope we're doing as well!'

The top rocked at the thundering reverberation of our own guns; the air was thick with the cordite smoke; the whistle and shriek of shells as they passed, hit, or burst short were as insistent as the noise of a railway engine's whistle in a tunnel; sheets of spray were wafted up to them and fell like waterfalls without making any distinguishable sound; whilst, as he caught sight of them between the showers, the rangefinder's voice, all trace of excitement gone, went on with its monotonous sing-song: '17,000 – 16;500 – 15,000.'

For a second the officer glanced at the ships in front. Even as he turned, he saw three enemy shells falling on the next ahead.

For an appreciable space of time it seemed as if the salvo had failed to take effect. Then suddenly every sense was staggered and shocked by an explosion so near and so violent that it seemed to come from their own ship and compelled an involuntary glance beneath them where their hull showed firm and solid. From the ship ahead an appalling column of smoke and flame shot up in the air to a height of 800 feet and then opened out into a screen, completely masking their vision ahead. Underneath this pall, and travelling so rapidly towards them that it was throwing up a bow wave, the stern of the stricken ship suddenly appeared and looked as if it were going to run into them although a second before it had been travelling at the speed of 26 knots in the opposite direction. Just as collision with it seemed inevitable the stern dived into the depths and sank so rapidly that although the following ship must have passed over it it did not touch. Just after the explosion the concussion of the water struck the *Tiger* so violently that it felt as if she had been torpedoed.

In the conning tower the catastrophe had been seen and an effort was made by swinging the helm over to prevent the ship from overrunning the wreck. The result of this sudden helm was to heel the ship bodily to one side, and whilst she was in this position the heel was exaggerated by the mountainous wave thrown up by the explosion, so that it seemed to those in the top that their ship must go right over.

Prompt though the action of the navigator had been, it was impossible in that short distance to clear the wreck entirely and she must have passed over the main part of the hull as well as the stern. But so instantaneous was the disappearance that no evidence was ever found of her having touched the submerged hull.

In spite of the efforts to avoid it the battle cruiser slid into the dark cloud of blinding hot smoke and there was the rattle of debris of every description on the light steel plating which formed the roof of the top, while the decks were strewn everywhere with fragments as they fell like rain from the sky. In less than a minute the ship was in bright sunlight again, she was on an even keel and, except for the debris on the deck, a few fragments of floating wreckage in the water, and a dark cloud astern in the sky, all trace of the *Queen Mary* and her 1,300 men had disappeared.

The *Tiger* went ahead and took up her station in the line astern of the flagship to fill the place of the missing ship.

The voice of the man at the range-finder again took up the refrain: '15,000 – 14,500 – 14,000.'

The hulls of the enemy ships were now plainly visible, but the range was still too great for the secondary armament to be of any value against the thickly armoured sides of the German ships. Would they never come any nearer? As if in reply to his question, he suddenly saw a line of low black hulls emerge from behind the enemy ships and come tearing in a line diagonally towards him.

Here was work at last! Seizing the navyphone, he shouted down to the captain: 'Destroyer attack on the port bow. Request permission to open fire.' The reply came back: 'Open fire at 10,000.'

Dropping the navyphone, he picked up the voice tube and commenced the orders to the transmitting station, which would let loose 6,600 pounds of shell per minute at the rapidly approaching enemy:

'Destroyer. One mast, two funnels.'

'Range 9,500. Deflection 16 right. Rate 550 closing.'

'Load with lyddite. Salvoes.'

'Shoot!'

Anxiously he gazed at the leader of the approaching destroyers. Good shooting, but a little to the left. Undoubtedly she was hit or, at least, badly spattered, as she altered course a little. Correcting this, he shouted down:

'Shoot!'

Again the deadly hail smothered the little vessel in foam. From the top the men on her decks could be clearly seen training the torpedo tubes and getting ready to fire. As she approached, the order was given:

'Down 400. Shoot!'

There was a sudden burst of speed on the part of the destroyer, which was immediately allowed for.

'Down 400. Close rate 200. Rate 750 closing. Shoot!'

'Good hunting!' he muttered, as the destroyer swerved in her path and, apparently badly injured, commenced to alter her course so as to get out of action.

Smoke and flame were belching from her forward, whilst amidships a ragged hole in her side could be seen from which great clouds of steam came out in gasps. She was heeling towards him, and the crew could be seen plainly through glasses, fitting on their life-belts and dragging at the falls of their badly damaged whaler. Rafts were being cast loose, and the deck was strewn with bodies which, even as they watched, commenced to roll slowly down the sloping deck.

'Not much need to worry about him!' thought the lieutenant. 'He's finished. Time to get on with the next.'

The second destroyer had been attended to by the ship astern, but the third was still coming on, apparently uninjured. She was rapidly altering both course and speed in order to avoid the deadly salvoes and spoil the range-finding.

'Oh, that's your game,' said the officer. 'We'll see what we can do for you.' Speaking down the voice-pipe again, he shouted: 'Object shifted. Third destroyer from left. Range 8,500. Same deflection and rate. Salvoes. Shoot!'

All-overs was reported by the spotter.

'Down 400. Shoot!'

'One hit, others short!' shouted the spotter.

'Up 200. Shoot!'

There was no need to listen to the spotter this time. The middle of the destroyer rose in the air and then burst asunder. With a roar, she broke in halves, and bow and stern were elevated skyward until she assumed the shape of the letter V. Almost instantaneously she disappeared. As she did so, she went straight downwards as if plucked under by a gigantic hand. The fourth destroyer put her helm hard over and turned sixteen points. She had been hit once by the ship astern and had evidently had enough.

The lieutenant chuckled. 'Gave Fritz what-for that time! Guess our destroyers could have done better than that!'

'Cease firing!'

For the time being, the destroyer attack had been foiled, but others were sure to come, and, smothered in spray, the men on the top kept anxiously on the alert. As they looked ahead, they saw first one, then another, then several separate clouds of smoke on the horizon. The German battle cruisers were heading straight for them, and the meaning of that was all too plain. Evidently these distant vessels were the German High Seas Fleet. The range of the German battle cruisers was rapidly getting less, and it was possible to start shooting at them with the secondary armament with a fair chance of hitting.

The lieutenant began to give his orders again, after asking permission from the captain. And, busy and capable as he was professionally, another part of his brain was speaking to his inner consciousness. 'This is *Der Tag* at last. Thank heaven we're in it. Verdun must have been a failure. Where is Jellicoe? We can't take on all these beggars by ourselves! Wonder how long Beatty is going to carry on. Their guns are badly rattled: they haven't hit us a fair smack for over an hour.'

The rapidly advancing High Seas Fleet was approaching the parallel lines of fighting battle cruisers. Still Beatty held on. But the lieutenant had no doubts in his own mind. 'Jellicoe can't be far away, and we are going to hold them until he comes up. May it be soon!'

Still the battle cruisers held on, while the German battleships commenced firing at long ranges.

At last the signal to go about was given, and the helm was jammed hard a-port, so that the big ship heeled heavily over as she spun round. As she did so, it was obvious enough that the German battle cruisers were doing the same thing and racing back in the direction they had come. They had apparently got the idea that Beatty was trying to avoid them and was suffering too much punishment to be able to reply effectually. But that officer had his own game to play and knew as soon as the German battle cruisers turned immediately after him that they had fallen into the very error he had desired them to make.

The Fifth Battle Squadron had now joined up and was engaging both the enemy's cruisers and battleships, and, as far as the battle was concerned, the day was now more in favour of the British.

As the ships swung round, one after the other, keeping perfect stations as if at manoeuvres, they fired their broadsides with telling effect, which was plainly seen, at the German battleships, but they responded indifferently.

It was easy for those in the top to guess what Beatty's tactics were. Evidently, Jellicoe was somewhere up in the northwest, and the whole German Fleet was walking straight into his hands. If only the light would hold! But already, although it was barely 5 p.m., the horizon was becoming misty and the outlines of the enemy ships were no longer sharply defined. To control effectively this long length of battle line, good light was absolutely essential.

Still Beatty sped along, keeping station on the German cruisers at 18,000 yards, leaving their battleships to the Fifth Battle Squadron. The Germans by this time were suffering heavily, and the *Lutzow* was seen to drop out of the line.

Suddenly, ahead on the port bow, were seen the welcome signs of the Grand Fleet arriving at last. There was no longer any doubt as to what the result would be. Inevitable defeat was staring the Germans in the face. With the instinct of the born fighting sailor, Beatty seized the chance to turn the

German defeat into a rout. The battle cruisers leaped ahead at full speed and he dashed like a fury across towards the head of the German line in order to concentrate on their leading ships and crumple their formation. The manoeuvre was perfectly successful. The German line bent, broke and fled, but the thick mist which had gradually been coming down robbed Jellicoe of the fruits of his victory. As the Grand Fleet deployed into line and brought their guns to bear on the enemy's line, they found for target an occasional wraith-like hull appearing for a few seconds between the banks of smoke and fog. The battle cruisers were in the same quandary, firing at intervals at the flashes which showed the position of the German ships. The utmost confusion apparently reigned on board them, and in the thick fog and scattered condition of both fleets, to go on with the action was impossible.

Once again, as often before, the weather conditions had favoured the defeated, and both fleets mutually broke off action – the Germans to flee for their home ports, and the British to re-form for the battle at dawn.

During the night, that best test of the morale of a fleet, a destroyer attack, was carried out by the British with marked success; but there was no retaliation on the part of the Germans. They had had enough and more than enough.

At 10.30 p.m. a group of stiff and wearied officers left the top and made for the wardroom to get some food. The forsaken afternoon tea was still standing as it had been left on the table and lying about on chairs, sofas and settees, were men too wearied even to desire to eat.

They sat and looked at one another and said nothing. Members of the mess who had been joyfully skylarking eight hours before would never draw their chairs up to the table again. One who had left his cup of tea untasted had drunk to the dregs the cup that Death had offered him. Only one officer made the remark: 'The action is to be resumed at dawn.' And only one man made a reply: 'They won't get away this time.'

But they did. A Zeppelin was sighted at 3.30 a.m., evidently shadowing the British Fleet. For ten hours they cruised over the battle area strewn with the horrible relics of the fight, but the Germans were nowhere to be seen. They had gone home to celebrate their victory by getting their wounded into hospital, their dead buried, and their sunken ships renamed.

Chapter X
The M.O. in Action

'Action Stations' have just gone, and from my position on the platform under the bridge I take a look around before going below to my billet. It is a lovely May afternoon with a warm sun shining delicately through the haze; there is a smooth sparkling sea and a peaceful sky. On every side can be seen the ships of the Battle Cruiser Fleet, and from the smoke pouring from their funnels and the increasing vibration under my feet I know that we are working up to full speed. Deep down in the bowels of my own ship some 700 men are stoking, oiling, tending auxiliaries in a scene of ordered activity with just a suspicion of excitement. On deck, except for a small group of officers outside the conning tower in which they will shortly take shelter, there is nobody to be seen except myself. But in the barbettes, where the guns are being elevated and depressed while the turrets swing, keen-eyed men are scanning gun sights, and within the battery the crews have manned the six-inch guns. Up in the fighting top are the gunnery and torpedo experts and the range finders, who, with the occupants of the conning tower, are the only men on board who will have any real idea of how the action is going. Out of our ship's company of 1,500 men, perhaps 50 will get any view of the fighting at all. I am not one of them.

A glance ahead shows on the horizon to the eastward half a dozen widely separated wisps of smoke ascending in the still air. No hulls or funnels are to be seen from the level at which I stand, but from the fighting top they have already been

THE M.O. IN ACTION

recognised and named as the enemy battle cruisers. I know that the range is closing and that in less than half an hour these ships and ours will be doing their utmost to destroy one another, to mangle and murder, to rend souls from tortured quivering flesh. I am no pacifist or any other kind of 'ist,' only a plain medical man who has tried throughout his life to lessen suffering wherever he has found it, and here are two nations who think they can settle their quarrel by inflicting an infinity of suffering against which the efforts of a hundred like myself are useless. The stupidity of it!

Time to go, and as all the watertight hatches are closed and the ladders have been removed I pass down through the only channel left, and by way of the signal distributing station and perpendicular steel permanent ladders I drop down and down until I am well below the ship's waterline. Along a narrow passage between steel bulkheads I come to the Medical Officer's station, the lineal descendant of the old cockpit of Nelson's day. With the usual tendency of the service for misnomers, it is called the Medical Officer's distributing station. He does distribute ambulance parties from it, but its main function is to collect and treat the wounded during action.

My station is a circular space formed by the casing which supports the weight of 'B' barbette with its armoured hood and brace of 13.5 guns. Picture to yourself this circular space divided fore and aft and athwartship by steel bulkheads into four wedge-shaped compartments a considerable area of which is taken up by the ammunition hoists passing from the magazines under our feet to the guns above. The diameter is about 25 feet and from this measurement an idea of the size of the rooms can be guessed.

I enter the first apartment by means of a doorway without any door but a very high coaming to step over: the size of the doorway being almost exactly that of the body of an average sized man, as I am to find out later to my cost. This room communicates with the forward and starboard rooms by a similar doorway, and the latter again opens into its own forward room. In these four spaces I have to receive the dead and wounded, dress and treat the latter, and keep my stretcher parties in safety as long as they are not required for duty.

The after starboard compartment is rigged up as a small operating theatre, and there is an operating table, an electric fan, taps for cold water and an electric apparatus for heating it; and of course the usual tools of my trade. In one corner is a telephone, by means of which I can communicate with any other part of the ship. There is, of course, no daylight, but the electrical system is ample for my purpose.

We have water, light and air; but as all these are artificially supplied we may at any moment lose any one or all of them; so in case the water goes we have spare buckets full, standing about in the compartments. For spare light there are small portable battery lamps which can be hooked to a waistcoat button so as to throw its light on your work and leave the hands free. For air – well there is no way of supplying air. A shell exploding in a confined space drives out the normal air contents and leaves in its place the irrespirable gases, gases manufactured by the process of explosion. It is a horrid feeling to be semi-suffocated whilst all the time you have no difficulty with the mechanical act of respiration. To protect the bronchial mucous membrane from the inflammatory effect of acrid fumes we have small gauze respirators which have been soaked in a soda solution. Poison gases in the ordinary acceptance of the term are not used in naval warfare. In case of disaster to the ship there is no possible escape from the station.

For my staff there are two junior medical officers and six sick-berth ratings. In action, however, some of the so-called 'idlers,' i.e. men who do not keep a watch, are turned over to

THE M.O. IN ACTION

my department to act as stretcher bearers and dressers. They are domestics, messmen, cooks, waiters and ratings from the Paymaster's department, about twenty all told. Also in each barbette and casemate there is a trained ambulance man with a first-aid outfit, and in the engine rooms and stokeholds there are ratings who have been trained in the treatment of burns and scalds.

The two junior officers are what we called 'temporary' surgeons. One of them told me he was so temporary that it had become a habit.

There are eight stretcher parties skilled in first aid and supplied with a flexible cane stretcher, the invention of an ingenious naval medical officer. This is the exact length of a man and it can be bent round corners. When the patient is wrapped up in it he can be hoisted or lowered from deck to deck in almost any position. Most of these ambulance men have had two years of intensive training and they are keen and capable. Not the least difficult and lengthy part of their training has been instruction in the geography of the ship. Not one of these men fails to indicate at once the most direct alternative route to the cockpit should the usual approach be blocked. The courage and devotion shown by these ambulance parties in carrying out their dangerous and often horrible duties is beyond all praise. And when I say horrible, I mean just that. It must be clearly understood that the first duty of the medical department when the ship is fighting is not the care of the wounded, but to ensure that the dead and wounded do not interfere in any way with the fighting efficiency of the ship. There is no need to dwell on the ghastly scenes which the fulfilment of this duty entails.

As I enter the inner room the senior of the two medical officers reports 'Ambulance parties present and correct, Sir!' and together we wander round the four compartments to see whether any last-moment improvements in our arrangements are advisable. One of the compartments, the starboard forward one, is entirely given up to tiers of canvas cots or troughs in which four men can lie alongside one another. In the other compartment are cots spread on the deck. In the entrance compartment the cases are roughly overhauled, their names and ratings taken by a writer, and their clothing examined for money and valuables. In one case we found £15 on the flannel of a dead man.

Back in the operating room I speak to two other officers who, having no special duties in action, have volunteered to help me. One is the Chaplain, who has been dragged from the care of fashionable souls in a well-known London church to be set down amongst us who have no respect for his cloth as such, but have learned to appreciate the man behind the dog collar. The other officer is the Paymaster-in-Chief, probably the oldest man on board the ship and entitled by his age and standing to shore billets, which he contemned. He had seen fighting when most of us were in long clothes, if we existed at all, and nothing could keep him away from a ship as soon as he knew there was to be a war. During the long winter months of our two years at sea he had been my greatest friend. He spent most of his time dressing trout flies with more than professional skill, so as to be in readiness for the fishing that never came. He died shortly after the War – a very great gentleman.

A roaring noise overhead, a violent concussion which shook everybody and everything in the compartment, and our 13·5's were speaking. This was to go on every four minutes for over two hours, but it was not to be the dominating feature for long. There was a crash and a shiver along our port side just abaft the cockpit, and then the concussion of a bursting shell.

The immediate alteration in the air pressure round about our confined space first made breathing difficult, and then there was the shrieking of a thousand whistles in every key as the violently compressed air passed through numberless crevices. The ship reeled from the blow ever so little, and then ensued the old familiar noises overlaid by the thunder and shake of the guns overhead and the rattle of the ammunition hoists.

A call at the telephone and immediately the order 'Away all ambulance parties, port wing passage.' We had been badly hit and the shell, penetrating the decks, had burst at the cockpit level and killed and wounded many men as well as setting the ship on fire. There was some confusion outside the station, as the fire parties were connecting up the hoses to the hydrants just outside whilst the ambulance parties were beginning to bring in the wounded.

Hearing the din I went to the doorway and stood in it whilst giving orders for easier transport. Just then another shell pierced the decks and burst on our deck again just forward of the station. The whole width of the circular casing protected me from the direct impact of the explosion, but I was in the position of the pop in the popgun: the compressed air in front hurled me backwards into the negative pressure of the compartment behind me. Sick, giddy and stupid I struggled to my feet whilst the attendants rushed to my assistance. After a bit I felt better and was astonished to find I was unhurt except for a little bruising, although for the rest of the night I had attacks of faintness and sickness. Had I been outside the doorway instead of standing in it I should not have felt anything at all.

Meanwhile there was work to be done and plenty of it. The two junior medical officers were examining the wounded. In many cases a glance was sufficient, but others were living though badly injured. By the merciful dispensation of Providence, who has supplied the kindly shock for the alleviation of severe injuries, as yet they feel but little pain. Surgery of any systematic kind was out of the question as long as the concussion of our own guns continued. All that was possible was first aid of the most temporary character, and the more serious cases were put on the operating table for me to deal with – the Paymaster standing opposite me and assisting.

Suddenly, like all our happenings, there was a violent thud, undoubtedly coming from a blow struck under the waterline. The ship, which had hitherto been travelling on a perfectly even keel, slowly heeled over to port, and with a sickening movement hung on her side in such a position that the patient began to slide off the table and push me backwards with him. The Paymaster leant over from his side to help me and the same thought flashed through both our minds. We had been torpedoed and the ship was going to turn turtle. For a moment my friend caught my eye, and there was the same kindly twinkle in his which he used to show when I had praised some of his handiwork. 'Well, good-bye, Muir,' he whispered, and such was his look of perfect calm bravery and assurance that in spite of myself I gave a sheepish grin back. As we still looked at one another and the ship still hung as if uncertain whether to go over or not, the only feeling I was conscious of was an intense curiosity as to what was going to happen. Slowly, and as if painfully, the great ship returned to an even keel, and we fell to work again. I thought we had got it that time, was the Paymaster's only remark. We were to learn later that what we had experienced was the concussion and tidal wave thrown up by the explosion and instant disappearance of the *Queen Mary*.

Still the work went on. Time disappeared or seemed to stand still. There never had been any other life except this noise, this being hit and the consequent casualties, this unbreathable atmosphere. One patient was placed on the table, a swift description of his injuries noted down, his name if possible verified, a tally attached to him and his dressings completed. Then after a morphia injection he was carried off and deposited somewhere, whilst his place on the table was taken by another torn fragment of humanity.

At one time I heard a voice at my elbow saying 'Here's Shorty, Sir! He's badly hurt,' and a dying man dropped a limbless trunk at my feet. The heroism of that dazed mind which, itself in the throes of death, could only think of his chum as being so much the more badly injured of the two, and had borne him up in his struggle with his burden through the torn and twisted steel of the darkened alleyways, was something to give rise to awe and wonder. A minute after he had spoken there was nothing to be done for either except to let them join the melancholy heap which was gradually accumulating in an outside passage.

For some little time the firing of the guns overhead had been getting more and more desultory, only an occasional round at irregular intervals warning us that the action was still going on. The incessant stream of wounded had almost stopped, though every few minutes an injury from the turrets, or some other position from which the wounded could not be moved during the heat of action, was still arriving. We had no idea what was happening on deck or how the action had gone, nor had we received the faintest hint of our losses. The dressing station was a shambles; many of the cases urgently required operative treatment and all of them wanted nursing and attention to their various needs. All such treatment was impossible as long as our guns continued to fire.

After a distinct lull which had lasted for about half an hour I tried to get the Commander on the telephone, to ask him whether the action was over. After considerable difficulty the exchange operator managed to run him to earth.

'S.M.O. speaking.'

'Yes, what do you want?'

'I've got a whole lot of wounded here who need operative treatment. If the action is over I should like to start at once. Can you tell me anything?'

'I can't tell you anything about that. All I know is that this damned ship is on fire and I'm trying to put it out.'

'You're a devil of a lot of comfort,' was my answer, at which he chuckled through the telephone.

So that was the reason for the horrible atmosphere down below which I had expected to clear a little as I knew we had not been seriously hit for some time. Again there was the violent concussion of our big guns firing, but it did not last long this time. Someone said it was about 9 o'clock. We had been fighting since 3.30; we were all tired, dirty, half suffocated with the foul air from exploding shell, fires and damaged air circuits; I was still being sick at intervals; there was an appalling amount of work to be done.

One does not worry the Captain with minor details when an action is going on, but as the ship had been perfectly quiet since the last fusillade I rang him up on the telephone. A quiet, collected voice answered me and I told him my difficulty. He asked:

'Are our casualties very heavy?'

'Not very heavy;' and I gave him a rough estimate of the dead and wounded as far as I knew it.

'I think the action is over for the night, but I have no definite instructions. I shall let you know immediately I hear anything. Better hang on for a little before you start doing anything.'

Two minutes later there was a ring on the telephone.

'Signal from Flag.' I forget the exact wording of that rousing message from Sir David Beatty, but the end of it was what was of most importance to me at the moment. 'The action is to be dis-continued, but we hope to meet the enemy and resume the action at 3.30 a.m.' Immediately afterwards the bugle sounding the 'Pack Up' was heard and my temporary staff disappeared to take up their ordinary duties.

There were many wounded to be seen to, such surgery as was necessary to be carried out, food, water and dressings to be supplied, and quarters to be found for our cases. And it had to be finished somehow or other before 3.30 when we must be prepared for another lot of the wounded we were bound to get when the action was resumed. Could we do it?

I made a dash to the main deck to have a look at the beautiful Sick Bay where all the work could be done with the minimum of discomfort to the wounded. And as I made for the door, which was closed, a bluejacket stopped me.

'Look out where you are going, Sir! The Sick Bay is wrecked.'

It was just as well he spoke, since if I had stepped over the doorway to switch on the lights I should have fallen 30 feet to the bottom of the ship, where 600 tons of water were swishing about in our forehold. A flashlight showed a complete wreck of the whole compartment and a hole in the floor through which a motor car could be driven. There was no help here, and with action probable at 3.30 a.m. there was no chance of improvising a hospital in any other part of the ship. Back to the dressing station I went to make the best of it we could.

One of the surgeons to give the anaesthetic and the other to assist me, and the dreadful work began. One by one the poor shattered remnants were placed on the table, to find some moments of ease and peace under the anaesthetic; their injuries were dealt with as rapidly and thoroughly as possible, and then accommodation was found for them in hammocks, cots or mattresses spread on the deck or laid out on mess-tables. All the time we worked feverishly, so as to be ready for the fresh casualties at 3.30. We had no conception of time or how it was passing, but when the last urgent case was on the table I noticed that he was not completely under the anaesthetic, and without lifting my head from the job I was doing I protested.

'Can't you keep him under? How the devil can I do anything properly while he is wriggling about like this?'

There was no answer, and I looked round at the boy who was acting as anaesthetist. He had dropped off his stool and was lying on the floor sound asleep. He had anaesthetised himself.

Time to call a halt! With the aid of a sick berth rating the case on the table was finished and I asked the time. '5.30,' was the answer. We had been operating since 9.30 p.m. Evidently there was to be no resumption of the action for the present. The Germans must have got away again.

Earlier in the night I had received a message from the Captain saying he didn't want to bother me about official reports until such time as I could spare easily. As, I knew there would be anxiety about our casualties amongst the folks at home, I made up my list of dead and wounded and climbed up to the bridge to hand it over to the Captain. Here a grey-faced man was standing looking across to where, close at hand, the bows of the *Invincible* were standing straight up out of the sea. A little away and not so easily recognisable was her stern. Round the ship in every direction could be seen the ghastly relics of the fight. The Captain listened gravely to my report, expressed his deep concern at the numbers of the casualties, and gave me *carte-blanche* to use any part of the ship I wanted for the accommodation of the wounded. Also if there were no more fighting, and he did not think there would be, I could have any assistance I required.

Tired and feeling wretchedly seedy, as I was still being sick in spasms, I thought I would slip into the navigator's cabin under the bridge. This was a regular meeting ground for the senior officers, who were always sure of a welcome and a yarn from its cheery owner. Although entirely unprotected by armour it had escaped damage, and the scuttles were open although the deadlights were still hanging down over them, making a dim restfulness from the glorious sunlight of the morning outside. On pushing aside the curtain I could not see any occupant, but stepping forward to seat myself in a comfortable armchair I saw an officer, whose face I did not recognise, looking at me. I went forward to speak to him, to find I was looking at my own reflection in a mirror. I subsided into the armchair to rest for a little and must have dozed off, because I was suddenly startled to hear the voice of our Engineer Captain saying 'Good God! There's one of them in here.' In the dim light he had thought I was a dead body stretched out in the chair. However, he was soon assured that I was not so dead as I looked. He gave me a brief account of our terrible ship losses and after a short talk we both left the cabin.

Now that it was not likely the action would be renewed – in fact we shortly got news from the Admiralty wireless that the German Fleet had eluded us and returned to its bases – it was possible to improvise hospital accommodation, and the Captain's lobby and various other airy parts of the main deck were pressed into service. The work entailed in attending to the helpless wounded was very heavy and fell almost entirely on the shoulders of my six sick-berth staff and the two junior medical officers. There were some thirty men who were quite unable to do anything for themselves; their wounds required frequent dressing; they had to be washed, fed and cleaned; and their sanitary arrangements alone meant about 120 visits in the twenty-four hours. It was unlikely that we could be back at our bases and able to transfer our wounded to the hospital ships for at least thirty-six hours, and our arrangements were calculated accordingly. Unfortunately our wounded were accommodated in small batches in widely separated parts of the ship, and this entailed much extra labour in nursing.

The spirit of the wounded was wonderful. Although I fear there was often plenty of justification for it, there was never any murmuring or complaints. With the means at our disposal the nursing and general attention could only be of the roughest description, and there was much suffering and discomfort which a little less battle damage in my own department would have avoided. The nearest approach to a complaint I heard came from a fine young artificer whose right arm I had been compelled to amputate at the shoulder during the night. When dressing it during the next day, he looked at the stump and then actually half smiled at me. 'Seems hardly worth while this fighting, Sir!'

Our wounded have been attended to but there is still something to be done for those who are past all help. It is both fit and proper that the seaman who dies or is killed in action at sea should be buried in a sailor's grave. The bodies have been reverently collected and, after identification (no easy task in some cases), placed in one of the six-inch gun casemates. There the sailmaker and his mates have spent the day stitching up the remains in their hammocks with a round shot at their feet. A signal has been made that all the ships will bury their dead at the same time, and about five in the afternoon the officers and men fall in on the quarter-deck for the burial service.

It is a grim scene. The afternoon is dull and grey with a little wind whipping the sandy water into a frothy yeast. The ships are zig-zagging, and as they alter course we can see our consorts with the scars of battle showing clearly, each with its funeral party mustered on the quarter-deck. Along the whole length of the starboard side of our own deck, lying on gratings with their feet pointing outward, are our dead, the human shape scarcely recognisable under the coarse canvas covering. The stanchions which usually protect the quarter-deck have been lowered so as to leave a free passage over the ship's side. At the head end of each grating stand two bluejackets whose duty it is to perform the last rite for their mess-mate.

THE M.O. IN ACTION

The ensigns of the Fleet are half-masted, officers and men remove their caps, and the robed Chaplain begins the funeral service. The faces of all present are set in a stony stare looking anywhere except at that pitiful muster on the starboard side. At the words 'we commit their bodies to the deep' the seamen at the gratings lift up the head end, and the hammock with its contents slides with a sullen splash into the sea and disappears at once from sight. In peace time the ship would be stopped for a burial, but in war time no such action is possible. The funeral party is dismissed, the ensigns mast-headed, and our late messmates left to their lonely watch.

The Captain sends me a message. 'The Admiral wants your nominal list of casualties in order to wireless them to the Admiralty.' The list is ready, but before handing it in I think it as well to have it checked over again. The casualties are sent to the senior officer in each department and he is asked to verify and let me know the result over the telephone.

Whilst waiting for the results the senior engineer officer comes to my cabin.

'Look here! You've got the name of so-and-so down as killed. He's working in the stokehold now.'

'Wha-a-t! Are you sure?'

'Certain. I've just seen him myself. How did you identify him?'

'There was only one way to identify him and that was from the name stamped on his flannel.'

'Well, it must have been somebody wearing this other man's flannel. It's a common enough game to swop flannels.'

'For goodness sake muster your people and find out who's missing.'

'Yes; but there are 700 of them scattered all over the ship. It will take some time.'

It was done, however, and the dead man identified by a process of exclusion. But the incident spoiled my rest for some time when I thought of the close shave there had been of tolling a living man's relatives that he had been killed in action.

Meanwhile the care of the wounded went on unceasingly, and it was with a sigh of relief that, after a sleepless night, we entered the Forth. There everything was ready for us and the big hospital ships came alongside as soon as we were anchored, so saving the wounded from the suffering which transport in boats must have caused. In an incredibly short time they were transferred, and I was free to shave, wash, eat and sleep in peace.

But before that happened there was still something to do and I went to see the Commander about it. Like everybody else at sea, I was constantly pestered by souvenir-hunting friends for relics of our scraps. The other souvenir hunters had been busy immediately after the action whilst I had been otherwise engaged. So I had asked the Commander to get a memento for me.

'What about that souvenir you promised to get for me?'

'Well, old thing, I thought about you and kept something for you.'

'That was good of you! Hand it over.'

'As a matter of fact I left it on the upper deck.'

'What's it doing there?'

'Come up and have a look at it.'

I followed him into the battery. Standing in one corner was an almost complete German shell weighing, as we afterwards found, something over 700 pounds.

'There you are,' said the Commander; 'and a job I had to prevent the other people from sneaking it. You can take it away any time you like.'

'Thank 'ee kindly!' I said. 'Thank 'ee, and again thank 'ee.'

I believe it was finally deposited in the museum of the Royal United Service Institution.

Chapter XI
Aftermath

Two days later, battered and bruised but broken neither in spirit nor fighting efficiency, what remained of the battle cruisers approaches Rosyth once more. The battle of Jutland is fought and over, and without undue haste, as becomes the rulers of the seas, we are returning with our dead. Mourning our losses, but by no means cast down by them, we enter the narrow waters that lead to our base. We have carried out the duty for which we were born, trained and paid. That 6,000 of our friends and shipmates will never return to gladden the eyes of that silent, waiting crowd on the piers is the only message we shrink from delivering. We can feel, through the horrible stillness of our progress to our billets, how they con and recognise the ships as they pass. Gripped with deadly despair, they pray that the next ship may be their ship. 'Thank God! Thank God!' shouted one woman; 'that is the *Invincible*.' But it was the *Inflexible*. 'Where is the *Queen Mary*?' moaned another. 'Oh, where is the *Queen Mary*?' Ay, where?

These men were our past shipmates, our present friends, our future supports, bound to us by the all-powerful ties that link the lives of those who go down to the sea in ships. They had done their duty as they had lived, singly, simply and worthily and had fallen in no mean effort. Even amidst the unspeakable agonies of the water-tight compartments of the sunken ships, before the kindly hand of suffocation had eased their pain, we knew that they were content. We who, in all knowledge, had faced the same horrors and escaped to go back again and again to encounter them once more, knew well what we had done. Still in our ears were ringing Sir David Beatty's signal, made in the grey dawn of the 1st of June, 'We hope to meet the enemy to-day and utterly annihilate him. Every man must do his utmost.' We remembered the long cruise up and down amongst the ghastly relics of the battle area, hoping against hope, and the failure of that hope. The value of our work we had gauged from that cruise and the utter failure of the enemy even to attempt a destroyer attack during the night.

Victory! We were not out for the victories which please the children and adorn newspaper headings. We were out to prove to the German that at whatever cost to ourselves, he ventured upon the open seas at his peril. He had been taught his lesson, and had had it rubbed into him in a way his grandchildren will never forget. Is it victory to Germany to know that the seas are closed to him while one English keel remains to dispute it –that come he in power or weakness, the result is the same? ...

Our wounded are landed and our dead are buried, and we are free to go ashore for the short period the Service can spare us. We shrink from meeting our wives on the doorstep, lest the new-made widow next door may have her agony renewed at the sight.

And then the storm burst on our devoted heads. A simple, straightforward account of the action had been published by the Admiralty, to be greeted by the nation with wrath and uncomprehending dismay. With hearts swelling with anger, we note the pitying glances of the soldiers, who furtively look the other way and forget to salute us as we pass. In the streets of the local town we are hissed, for what do the men who guard the seas for the greatest maritime nation on earth deserve better? We have done our work and paid the price with our own bodies, but to this nation of shopkeepers the cost in ships is so excessive as to be worse than a cheaper defeat. Why didn't we run away and save our ships, when speed had been given us at great expense in order that we might do so? Why did Beatty attack the superior German Fleet? Why didn't he fall back on the Grand Fleet? Why didn't he do this, that and the other? In order, my parsimonious friend, that you might sleep in safety with your wife to-night.

It is all over and done with now, but – the Great Silent Navy does not easily forget. For the future we know that, as heretofore, we must do our work and hold our peace, leaving to history the kindly judgment our contemporaries have failed to give.

So it is better to pass over the memory of these days lightly, though they were full of bitterness to every individual in the Fleet. Here was the aftermath of the *Audacious* story in full measure, pressed down and running over. What are you fellows hiding? I was asked. If the Admiralty admit so much of Jutland when they lied so glibly about the *Audacious*, what are they concealing now? It was useless to say we were hiding nothing. The sure shield! And yet there was something we all knew, but we did not talk about it. We had gone into action believing we possessed the finest fighting ships afloat and that on the skill and courage we displayed depended the result. We expected losses and heavy losses, but were prepared to meet them at whatever cost to ourselves in lives and ships. We came out of action knowing that our ships were incompletely divided up and insufficiently protected, that our system of ammunition supply to our big guns was archaic, and wondering at the chance which had allowed us to return at all. The loss of our ships in the way that happened had been foreseen by our gunnery department long before, and they had fought the constructive department, on whom the responsibility of designing these ships fell, and had been defeated. Again and again it had been pointed out that side armour was a perfect protection against gunfire at close range when the trajectory was flat but that at the long ranges at which future naval actions would be fought the trajectory would no longer be flat but a well-marked parabola, with the projectile falling almost perpendicularly on its target. To counter this, such a ship as the *Queen Mary* had three-inch teak decks covering a thin steel plating – as much use against an eleven-inch shell as so much paper. What our ships needed was horizontal as well as lateral protection, and they had not got it. On our own ship the nine-inch steel armour plates on our side were pushed in sometimes as much as a foot by a shell without any real damage taking place; but if the shells dropped on our decks they passed through them and spread destruction everywhere. After Jutland steps were taken to remedy this want of protection and in our case two-inch steel plating was bolted down over the wooden upper decks. That thickness could not, of course, prevent the shell coming through, but it was believed the impact against the armour would explode the shell before it had penetrated far enough to do much damage. Whether it would have done so I do not know. We were never given any chance of finding out.

For a little we remained at anchor in case the Germans should wish to follow up Jutland with another demonstration, but as all seemed quiet we were ordered into dry dock for overhaul and refitting. This was an opportunity for ten days' leave, our first since July 1914. We returned to find that, owing to the extensive repairs required by the *Lion*, we were to act as Sir David Beatty's flagship, and for some six weeks we flew his flag. There could be little personal contact; and that only of the briefest possible description, between the Admiral and his Senior Medical Officer, but it behoves me here to say that not a single suggestion of the so-called Beatty-Jellicoe controversy ever reached our ears. The Fleet as far as I know never adversely criticised the tactics of either of these leaders.

AFTERMATH

As far as we were concerned, Beatty had carried out the duty expected of him. He had fought the enemy battle cruisers, shepherded their battle fleet into the arms of the Grand Fleet and, having crossed the 'T' for them, his work was done. The rest was Jellicoe's job. If the 'T' had been crossed a couple of hours earlier we knew what would have happened, but night was falling and with our enormous battle line the prospects of a night action implied greater risks than could legitimately be run when the chances of bringing the enemy to action at daylight were so good. So Jellicoe made his famous decision and the rest of the Fleet loyally accepted it until the paper tacticians had their say. Jellicoe did not know, and could not know, that his dispositions for intercepting the enemy at daylight had been foiled by the enemy wireless picking up a message from our own Admiralty and sending it to Scheer.

Whilst we acted as Flagship I only heard the Admiral make two criticisms which might be remotely connected with Jutland. At dinner one night one of the guests remarked that he had seen in the papers that the German Chief Naval Constructor had been awarded the Iron Cross. 'Somebody should give ours an Iron Mask – and make him wear it!' was the reply, recalling an earlier criticism on a more strenuous occasion: 'There must be something wrong with our ruddy ships, Chatfield.' On another occasion at the end of a war game which was played on board our ship, the Admiral summoned all the officers who had been taking part in the game to listen to his criticism of the results. 'When visual signalling is impossible and the, wireless is jammed, some officers seem to be in doubt in which direction I am likely to turn. I want it to be clearly understood that I shall always turn towards the enemy.' This statement was considered by some as a possible allusion to Jellicoe's turning away movement at Jutland, but personally I don't believe it was anything but a simple statement of fact. David Beatty always would turn towards the enemy. In the psychological equipment of the ordinary man fear is an almost invariable factor. In Beatty fear just didn't exist.

About this time a good story was told about the Flag-Captain. For some months a controversy had been going on between two Commanders on board, the senior of whom was on the Admiral's staff whilst the other was the duly appointed Commander of the ship. The point was which, in case of the death of the Captain, should succeed him in command of the ship. It was a question which the two junior officers considered should be settled once for all, and they finally agreed to lay it before the Flag-Captain for his decision. Their statement was carefully listened to, but a decision in favour of either was difficult, and the Captain wished to avoid it if possible. So putting on his most aggrieved air he addressed them. 'I consider it absolutely inhuman of you two fellows to wrangle like this over my dead body.' The abashed officers faded away.

One more contact with the enemy was made during August, the importance of which was the realization it gave of the enemy's future tactics at sea. In response to a signal that the enemy fleet had put to sea and was cruising off his coasts, apparently bent on another raid, our Grand Fleet put to sea and swept that area. Following up the High Seas Fleet they were led into a submarine trap and we lost the *Falmouth* and *Nottingham*. It was obvious that the German Fleet had no intention of risking another action, and that any further movements of our ships in the southern parts of the North Sea would only provide sitters for enemy submarines.

So we settled down in our base at Rosyth broken only by a short visit to the Grand Fleet base at Scapa Flow. It was the first time we had been in the same anchorage with the battleships since December 1914, and as we entered the Flow every ship in the anchorage was manned and cheered ship as we passed along their lines. It was the most thrilling moment of our lives.

One day our picket boat took me to the Flagship, but as it was urgently required for other duties, our Commander had asked me to send it back at once and recall it by signal as soon as my business was completed. But when I asked the Commander of the Flagship to let me send a signal for my boat his reply was 'Don't bother. I shall call one of our drifters alongside and you can go back in her.'

In less than five minutes a typical North Sea drifter was alongside the Flagship's ladder, and I tumbled down the side and stepped on board her. A soft-voiced Scotsman dressed in the uniform of a skipper R.N.R. met me and, as in Scapa Flow even in the middle of June the wind was keen, asked me to step into the little sheltered wheelhouse beside him whilst we cleared away from the huge battleship's side.

The voices around me were the voices of my northern countrymen, but there was nothing in the appearance of ship or crew to suggest her normal occupation of fishing. Smartly painted, scrubbed, and polished from stem to stern, her crew perfectly dressed in naval uniform, she was the direct antithesis of her hard work-a-day peacetime appearance.

As we pushed off, the hands in the bow and stern dropped their boathooks in their appointed places, the captain rang down to the engine room, and the little ship rapidly gathered way to her extreme speed of 9 knots into the Flow.

A quiet voice was speaking. 'They didna tell me where you wanted to go, Sir. Where is your ship?'

'*Tiger*,' I said. 'Battle cruisers.'

'Oh, man! Ye're in the battle cruisers! And you've just come back from Jutland. The *Tiger*! Eh! Eh!' and the soft voice faded as he spun his wheel to the direction indicated.

In a few minutes the ship was steady on her course and the skipper was eyeing me in a sort of wondering amazement for which I could find little reason. At length,

'Ye must have had an awfu' time.'

The answer was banal enough but I could think of no other.
'Oh, it wasn't too bad. We didn't have a fearful lot of casualties.'
'Aye! Aye! But the *Queen Mary* was just ahead of you.'

The tragedy of that holocaust when 1300 men went in one wild flash to their doom was still heavy upon us, and I sat silent with unseeing eyes, gazing out of the windows of the little deck-house and thinking of many things.

'Ye sit there, man!' broke in the skipper. 'Ye've been through all that and ye can tell me nothing? You've been daeing things – daeing things!'

'We've all been doing things,' I answered. 'You're doing things just as much as any of us.'

'Oh, aye! I've been daeing things, have I? Me! What am I daeing? Just trapesing wi' officers round the Fleet.'

The bitter contempt in the voice was heartrending.

'Somebody's got to do it,' I said. 'It's necessary work.'

'Aye! Somebody's got to do it,' was the dispirited answer, and he conned his ship down a line of light cruisers that lay in our course. Once clear he began again, gradually gathering vehemence as he spoke.

'Somebody's got to do it! Aye! But dae ye think it was for this I jined up at the beginning of the War? I thocht to myself if they'd just put a wee bit gun in the bows and gie me somebody who could fire that gun I could ha' done something. She's a fine wee ship, no' a better sea-boat in Scotland. We can gang to sea and keep the sea for weeks if we need to, and there's no weather that can drive us in. There's no' a square foot o' the North Sea I dinna ken as weel as the palm o' my hand. They wadna get any wrang positions frae me. But no! They wadna let me, and I havena had salt water on my decks for months. Its nae life for a seaman, this! An' if a submarine did sink us, well, it wad be better than ganging back hame to say we had been naething but a ferry boat a' through the war.'

AFTERMATH

What could I say? It was useless to talk about the risks and the inevitable end to this man who from his childhood up had pitted his skill and his tiny ship against forces infinitely more destructive and almost as pitiless as submarine warfare and had conquered and had come home clear-eyed and unafraid. He seemed to expect no. reply but gazed ahead at the rapidly approaching group of battle cruisers with an expression of unutterable regret.

'Which one is your ship, Sir?' The question and the tone were in complete contrast to his recent outburst. He was again the skipper of the passenger drifter.

'Third in the line. You will see her name under her stern in a minute.'

As we made a wide sweep to come alongside the ladder he suddenly gave vent to a gasp.

'Michty me, Sir! What is that on your ship's side?'

'That's where a German shell hit us and pushed one of the armour plates in about a foot.'

'It didna dae any other damage?'

'No, but plenty of others did.'

'Aye! Aye! A German shell! And that's what it is to be hit!'

We were almost alongside the ladder and I held out my hand as the drifter's engines went astern.

'Good-bye, Skipper, and thank you.'

'Good-bye, Sir, and I'm proud to have carried you. But eh! man! if I had only been there!'

The engine room telegraph rang and the drifter shoved off, the skipper saluting me as he went off 'trapesing round the Fleet.'

* * *

In September whilst we were lying at Rosyth one of those objectless air raids was made by German planes over

Edinburgh. We saw nothing of them and the damage they did could hardly have compensated them for the cost of petrol. The most important result of the raid as far as I could gather was the shock it gave to the sense of modesty of a certain young gentleman. At the height of the raid two young girl students who lodged in a flat in the suburbs were huddled in their dressing gowns at the window of their bedroom at the back of the flat and overlooking the washing greens. Suddenly a plane dropped a bomb on the green and did considerable damage to the washing. Panic-stricken and half blinded by the flash, the girls dashed shrieking into a front room where a youthful male was burning the midnight gas. Shocked beyond measure, the gentleman rose to his feet. 'Do you young women not know that you haven't got your clothes on?' This appeal to their moral sense effectually banished their terror, and shamefacedly apologising for their intrusion the girls withdrew. I hope later the youth became a leading light in the Church for which he was studying. He deserved the highest honours.

Chapter XII
Jack at War

If you were to ask the bluejacket what he thought of the German he would reply tersely enough that he was a blighter and, provided that he was not speaking to an officer or a padre, the epithet would probably be well adjectived into the bargain. This opinion was the result of mature consideration, and the word itself is the worst that Jack can apply to anyone he heartily disapproves of.

It was not so at the beginning. The first feeling was, curiously enough, one of rather sneaking fondness for the enemy. Jack did not care much for the violation of Belgian neutrality, as the idea conveyed very little to him, and when we entered the war on that score, all he thought was that we had a thundering good excuse – and lucky to get it, as otherwise we might have stood out, which would not have suited his book at all. Jack is a good sportsman and an enthusiastic boxer, and does not worry about excuses for a scrap. He never loves his opponent half so well as when he is busy altering the relative position of the other's nose and eyes, and he looks on a thick ear as a deformity to be proud of, whether it has been given or received. Provided the other fellow can send him to the Sick Bay for a week to repair damages he loves him like a brother, and spends his spare time in the dog watches getting wrinkles from his enemy, asking him to hit him in the same adjectival place again and again until he has mastered the knack of warding off the blow. He is always willing to allow the other fellow full marks, and is commendably modest about his own achievements, generally comforting the vanquished by the remark 'You weren't half in training, sonny!'

So, when the Fleet disappeared from Portland into the grey mists of the North Sea, Jack was ready for everything and anything that came along. At first he rather worried about the home folks, but as soon as the liberal Admiralty separation allowances were granted, he heaved a sigh of relief and felt that now he could get on with the work with an easy mind. The next game was to meet the enemy. This last did not prove quite so easy as Jack expected. The enemy seemed to be considerably chary about putting in an appearance in an above-water manner, and the only evidence of his existence was given by means of mine and submarine. These worried Jack not at all although they caused his officers considerable anxiety. Jack didn't quite like them – there was very little to be proud of in being sunk by an enemy you could not see – but he put up with them as being the feints of the weaker opponent.

Getting tired of waiting, Jack finally went to look for the enemy and fought the Battle of the Bight. From his point of view it was a delightful little affair and he was quite pleased with his part in it. It was scarcely strenuous enough in the big ships, but the little fellows had a good go and Jack cheered them on in the same spirit that he cheers a couple of the boys fighting on the mess deck. He heard tales about the enemy which rather worried him – that a rescued German had spat in the face of the commanding officer of his rescuer and had promptly been helped over the side by the captain's coxswain – and similar yarns about the grossness, surliness and arrogance of our prisoners; but he put this down as a rule to the supposed fact that these were not the real German sailors, but only newly joined conscripts. Besides, there are black sheep in every flock, and Jack, having been more or less the black sheep of his own family for years, came to the conclusion that the blackness attacked the enemy in this particular fashion.

The sinking of our three cruisers by submarine in the North Sea came on Jack with a shock. It wasn't very sporting, he thought, to have sunk the ships one after the other just because they were trying to rescue drowning men, and he would have dearly liked the Germans to show a little good blood by leaving one of the ships to pick up the survivors from the other two. Jack began to learn and understand that this was war to the knife, and that he could expect neither mercy nor consideration from the enemy. This was still more firmly impressed upon him as he learned a little later, when another cruiser went down, that the submarine squatted amongst his floating victims for two days in order to get a chance of torpedoing the ships that came out to clear the sea of corpses. This procedure on the part of a warlike nation profoundly disgusted Jack, and he utterly failed to justify it by any rule of conduct he was capable of conceiving.

In the meantime tales of atrocities committed by the Germans during their advance through Belgium commenced to pour in and were eagerly read and commented upon throughout the Fleet. From the first Jack was absolutely convinced that these crimes had been done to order, and this was the element which puzzled him most. Perfectly disciplined himself and understanding thoroughly the magnificent discipline of the German army as evidenced by the automatic successes of that wonderful march, the theory of black sheep could not be entertained for a moment, and to his angry surprise he decided that such things were done on purpose. The purpose he utterly failed to see, as such actions, instead of striking terror into his heart, would only have made him see red and sent him out to avenge them in the speediest fashion possible.

When, on December 16, 1914, he found himself out at sea, not to fight the German Battle Fleet but in order to catch and punish if he could the German cruisers who were occupied in the wonderful military achievement of bombarding Scarboro', Whitby and Hartlepool, his wrath knew no bounds. The stories of German atrocities became for Jack on that day a living reality. His disappointment at our failure to round up the enemy was frightful to witness, and it was a sore and angry Fleet that went back to our bases on the 17th. From that day on the German ceased to exist for Jack and a new personality in the nations of Europe was born – the Germhun. By that name alone he was designated in the British Fleet, and the name will stick long after the present personnel is gathered to its fathers.

The routine of war-time did not press very heavily during the first few months. There was considerable excitement of one kind or another, and new harbours were constantly being visited as the German submarines found out the latest dispositions of the Fleet and made abortive attacks. To-day it is almost impossible to believe, when one considers the wonderful system of protection that was soon to allow our ships to lie at their bases in all the security of peace-time, that at the beginning of the War the British Navy did not possess a single suitable harbour for the Grand Fleet adequately protected against submarine and destroyer attack. The biggest want of success on the part of the German submarine service is that during this period of lack of protection they failed to take advantage of their opportunity. Whatever the real reason was, lack of knowledge of the inadequate defences, imperfect trust in the submarines, or unwillingness to risk their loss at the time when they had none too many of a good sea-going type, Jack only believed one thing, and that is that the German submarine service was suffering from cold feet. Certainly, had the same chances been vouchsafed the British submarine service, the German Navy would have been destroyed during the first month of the war. Thinking over these and many other things on which it is impossible to dilate, every bluejacket was incensed and amused at the suggestion that we were preparing for war before it broke out. Incensed, because if we were preparing, our preparations were the preparations of fools; and amused, because he knows what preparations were made and how stupidly the Germans overestimated them.

But, as it slowly dawned on the Fleet that the Germans had no intention of putting up a stand-up fight until at some problematical future period when the mine and submarine, and perhaps isolated actions, would have diminished our numerical but by no means at that time overwhelming superiority, Jack found himself confronted by a winter of nothing but weary watching. Not by any means a life of idleness, as probably three days out of five were spent at sea, and the two in harbour were spent in coaling, provisioning, drills and exercises. But recreation, especially hard physical exercise of some kind, is essential to the health and well-being of the British Tar, and our bases were almost useless for these purposes. The far-sighted senior officers, convinced from the first that it would be a long war, had started in at once to transform desert wastes into football fields and golf courses; small jetties for landing were built; huts and canteens erected on the grounds; and everything that forethought, experience and sympathy could suggest carried out.

But it was absolutely necessary that not a gleam of light should be allowed to emanate from a ship, as it might betray the whereabouts of the Fleet. In many, if not most of the ships, this could only be accomplished by lighting the upper mess decks by obscured lights which barely made the darkness visible and utterly negatived any games, reading or writing. In those northern climes where the sun sets at 3.30 p.m. and gives no light worth speaking about until 9 a.m., the misery of the life led on the mess decks can hardly be imagined. At the best of times Jack's floating home consists of 21 inches of wooden mess stool facing 21 inches of one side of a bare wooden mess table 2 feet wide. His bedroom consists of two hammock hooks about 11 feet apart, between which is the hammock. His day clothing is stowed in the hammock beside him. For recreation on some ships a small room about 20 feet by 12 feet is provided, fitted with the usual mess tables and stools. His worldly possessions are stowed in an iron locker about 20 inches cube.

For exercise he has the upper deck, absolutely unsheltered in any way, and the last place on earth one would choose in North Sea weather. To smoke he gets under the shelter of a screen on the upper deck. At sea in bad weather – and bad weather is the rule in the North Sea in winter – his mess decks are usually covered by about an inch of water, and his air, supplied through a tube, blows with a chilly blast that arouses a curse whenever he tries to make himself comfortable. There is not a chair with a back to it, much less an easy chair for him, throughout the whole length and breadth of the ship. There is no relaxation of discipline possible, morning, noon or night. Once the war started, he had not an hour's freedom away from the ship in the shape of leave, except on rare occasions when he was granted a few days' leave because the ship was in dock and for the time being unfit to take her place in the battle line. Landing parties, of course, were organised, and men are taken ashore for a walk and marched to and from the recreation fields, always under the supervision of an officer. On many days on account of weather, duties, or being at sea, even this small amount of shore-going was denied him, and it is no exaggeration to say that hundreds of men never set foot on solid earth for a year after the war started. It is impossible for a lower-deck rating to get even the smallest glass of beer except for the one bottle that is doled out to him on the ticket system when he visits the wet canteen ashore.

On the other hand, he is well fed, and as long as he can afford to pay for it, he is well clothed. There is no free issue of clothing for Jack. When he first joins up he is provided with a free kit, but all replacements are made at his own expense, the money being automatically docked from his pay by the paymaster. Fear-nought suits, sea-boots and oilskins are provided for him by the Admiralty, but ordinary uniform, caps, boots and underclothing are a heavy drain on his resources. At the beginning of the war various charitable organisations supplied jerseys, warm underclothing, mufflers and so on; but out of sight with charity is too often out of mind, and later on Jack found the fount of charity run exceedingly dry.

It is almost impossible to convey to the landsman an adequate idea of the conditions under which Jack lives. Use and wont cover a lot, and Jack is no beggar, and has not the foggiest notion of how to advertise himself. He contents himself with saying, 'Who would sell a farm and go to sea?' buckles on his wet clothing to go and keep four hours' watch in the wind and rain, and does his duty with a thinking sense of responsibility unknown to his class in any other walk of life. He is keenly alive to the fact that on him depends the safety of the ship, and he considers and usually finds that the excuse 'I thought it was my job' justifies any departure from routine he may consider necessary.

Withal Jack is no hero to himself. He is a plain, simple-minded man, trained from his boyhood to know his work and to do it without any 'grousing.' His language is totally inadequate to express his feelings, whence it is usually garnished with many strange oaths, the literal meaning of which is absolutely unknown to him. Of late years there has been a great improvement in this respect, but even now he will reply to a remostrance when his language is a bit thick, 'What the – do you mean by saying I'm – well swearing?' Drunkenness is not his vice although occasionally on shore it may be, for lack of other employment, his recreation. Generosity is his instinct, and children of all ages he loves. He has one ambition, and as a rule one only, and that is to get what he calls a 'drop of leaf,' and if, in the course of his service career, he is appointed for an appreciable time to a stone frigate, life has nothing better in store for him. The sea is his enemy, and he faces it calm-eyed, knowing that it is ever hungry for him and that death is for ever, in peace or war, lurking at his elbow. But he has taken his enemy's measure and believes that, with the aid of that eternal vigilance that is the price of safety at sea, he will finally wind up as a good old 'has-been' in a 'whitewashed cottage' on the beach. There is more truth than humour in the story of the retired petty officer who hired a small boy to call him every morning at 5.30 with the statement 'The Commander wants you at once on the quarter-deck,' so that he might have the luxury of replying 'Tell the Commander to go to the devil.'

Generally speaking, he has tremendous respect for, and confidence in, his officers; but this trust is never given blindly. The errors of the man at sea are plain for the initiated to behold, and Jack expects that his officers will know a great deal more than the men they command. No officer can shelter his ignorance behind the skill of his petty officers. He will be recognised at once as a fraud, and receive as a reward obedience but no diligence. And if the officer is not careful he will find his men taking charge of him. He had the deepest reverence and admiration for Jellicoe, and his love went out wholeheartedly to Beatty. He loves to spin the yarn about Beatty that, in the Battle of the Dogger Bank, he remarked 'I'm going up to the upper bridge. This place is overcrowded,' – meaning the protected conning tower – and remained on the exposed bridge for the rest of the action. And at the time of greatest strain and stress at Jutland, when big ships were sinking all over the seas, how Jellicoe is supposed to have sent the welcome message to the hard-pressed battle cruisers, 'You can stand off now; I'll do the rest.' The yarns are probably untrue or mangled versions of real occurrences, but to Jack they typified our youngest and oldest Admirals – the one all dash and the other all stern efficiency. Last of all, to sum up this analysis of Jack's character, he abominates a slacker.

Remembering his idiosyncrasies and the conditions under which he lives at sea in war-time, Jack's feelings as he settled down to the routine of readiness for action in the winter of 1914-1915 can be more readily imagined than described. The long hours of enforced evening idleness in semi-darkness had a woeful influence on his spirits. The letters written at this period were full of the same complaints. 'Why won't they come out and fight?' – 'They might just give us a show, and then we could go home and be happy together.' – 'It's precious dull for us up here with not even a scrap to cheer us up.' – 'Why don't they come out and earn their keep at the job they're paid for?' – 'Gawd bless the High Canal Fleet.' – 'The first five years of this war will be the worst.' – 'I hear that this war will last five years, and then we are going to get four days' manoeuvre leave.' They jested – but bitterly. A rumour went round that mouth organs were being served out to troops in the trenches, and in response to urgent appeals a flood of these instruments, as well as gramophones, concertinas and melodeons, overwhelmed the Grand Fleet. Jack is a most ardent musician of much vehemence and little skill, and these impromptu concerts on the gloomy mess decks were the most appalling torture that the wit of man could devise. In self-defence the officers of several ships began to guide this energy into proper channels, and several very good fife and drum bands were the welcome results.

But it was weary waiting for both officers and men, and despite every possible method of alleviation being adopted, young men developed furrowed faces and grey hairs, whilst in not a few cases the mental balance proved to be unequal to the strain. The proportion of sick was wonderfully low, less than one per cent, but the ill-effects of this sleepless vigil were to be noted none the less.

The action of the Dogger Bank on January 24, 1915, came as a welcome relief to the souls who looked forward to a scrap to cheer them up. It was Jack's first experience of a big action in home waters, and the spectacle of the sinking *Blücher* impressed the men deeply. It was death to the enemy viewed for the first time at close quarters and the scene brought no elation to Jack's mind, only a feeling of overwhelming pity and deep regret that his was the hand compelled to do this thing. One of them wrote afterwards: 'I was in the scrap at the Dogger Bank when the *Blücher* was sunk and we were called up to see her go down. I was sorry I came up. It seemed such a shame to sink such a magnificent ship, and when I saw the crew running over the ship's side and plunging into the water I felt like a wicked child who had gladly done something wrong and then was disgusted at the result.' On all sides expressions of relief were heard that the other ships had got away, and a pious hope expressed that they would not be so foolish as to come out again.

About this time the labour troubles on the Clyde and in Wales were the subject of much discussion on the mess decks. The idea that strikes, especially in such important industries as coal and shipbuilding are in war-time, could be justified for any reason whatsoever was received with angry incredulity. Rather unjustly Jack believes that there can be no possible hardship in any job where a man can go to his own home every night, and the wages that were being scorned were such as he knew he could never earn at sea, although he got as high up in his profession as he could. In one ship a large proportion of the complement consisted of Welshmen and R.N.V.R ratings from the Clyde. With a fine sense of vicarious justice the Welshmen went for the Scots, whilst the North-country men poured their invective on the Taffies. Words in nearly every case came to blows, and whilst the representatives of the affected districts settled their differences as to which was the more criminal, the remainder of their shipmates knocked the combatants' heads together. When the strike actually did come about recriminations ceased, and for days together the Scots and Welsh were ashamed to look their messmates in the face. The most frantic letters were written to their respective districts appealing to the strikers to cease their quarrelling, which could only result in the destruction of their brothers in khaki and blue. Amongst the Scots was a well known local union official, who wrote thus to the secretary of his Association:

'I am utterly ashamed of the attitude of my Association in joining in this strike. At present no strike is justifiable under any circumstances, and the sordid reasons for the present one are enough to disgust any man who has abandoned all his prospects in order to take part in the defence of his country. There is not a Scot on board this ship who is not bitterly ashamed both of his Association and the Clydeside workers. At a meeting of the R.N.V.R. held on board this ship to discuss the situation, we all unanimously agreed that nothing would give us greater pleasure than for this ship to be told off to escort 250,000 German soldiers to be landed on the Clyde. The only excuse for your action is the grossest ignorance of the peril our country stands in, but such ignorance at this stage of the war must be due to criminal folly.'

From several sources we learned afterwards that this letter did more towards settling the Clyde troubles than anything else, except the piece of poetry from the front entitled 'My Brother on the Clyde.'

Meanwhile the so-called blockade of Great Britain by German submarines had got under way and Jack watched the dastardly attacks on merchant ships and the drowning of their non-combatant passengers and crews with ever-increasing wrath and desire for vengeance. Balked by our anti-submarine tactics of their legitimate prey, the German Admiralty prostituted their fighting force to the level of pirates, and merciless ones at that. To say that they entered upon this work with zest is no exaggeration when one remembers the *Falaba*, and Jack was painfully conscious that at last he was viewing the German in his true light with the veneer of civilisation stripped off. Jack, who had never in his whole existence balanced his own life for a second against that of a drowning stranger, had now to stand by – no, not quite helplessly as the records at the end of the War showed – and hear of women and children being sacrificed in the one form of death which alone he fears – slow suffocation in mercilessly cold water. As horror was piled upon horror, appealing to him with a strength that the landsman cannot have the faintest conception of, a new Jack was born, a little older and a little sterner and more purposeful; no longer looking on warfare as a game of boxing where the referee will sharply call the offender to order, believing and hoping that he would stick to the rules of the game himself, but recognising that from the enemy the same tactics were to be expected as from an undesirable opponent who could not, or would not, fight fair; no longer pitying the dying enemy, but satisfied that he was making the best of a grim job when he cleared these pests from the sea; sternly resolved that his life was misspent unless devoted to the task for which he was called. No longer were there any desertions during leave so that he might enlist and get to the Front, because it was so dull waiting with the

Grand Fleet. With all solemnity as befitted the risks he knew the work must bring, and clear knowledge that he carried his life in his hand, he became resolved that whenever and wherever he met the enemy he must see this thing through.

It was in this spirit that he fought at the Battle of Jutland. There was no excitement and no skylarking as before other actions. Whatever the losses on our side might be, the Germans must be fought and held; whatever the cost, punishment must be given.

So, as the War progressed, the idea of fighting a worthy foe was abandoned. Jack was out to rid the seas of men who were unworthy of the name of sailor. For the 'Germhun,' in his judgment, was a 'blighter.'

Epilogue

The winter of 1916 was approaching and the old mess had almost entirely disappeared as the result of promotions, exchanges, sickness and death. Towards the end of the year I was told that the Director General wished to consult me about alterations in my department considered advisable as the result of battle experience. In his office the bushy grey whiskers and penetrating eyes were turned hostilely upon me as I made my suggestions. Then the blow fell.

'You are going to be relieved.'

'But why, Sir? I don't want to go to any other appointment. I'd much rather finish the War in the old ship.'

'You've been there too long. No officer should serve at sea continually for over two years.'

'What is going to happen to me?'

'You will be sent to barracks for six months for a rest, and then you will be appointed to another ship.'

'I'd hate that, Sir. Send me' – I had a flash of inspiration – 'to Wei-hai-wei!'

'I have no intention of relieving officers on distant stations during the War.'

'Then some of them are going to have a devil of a long wait, Sir.'

No answer. The little grey eyes were piercing me through and through.

'How much leave have you had during the past two and a half years?'

EPILOGUE

'Ten days, Sir, and twice up here to see you.'

'You will be discharged to barracks as soon as I can arrange for your relief.'

Two days after my return to the ship I was handed my appointment as medical officer in charge of Wei-hai-wei.

So I did not see the surrender of the German Fleet at Scapa Flow, and I was glad of it. Apart from the ethics of their submarine warfare, which was a source of grief and wonder to all of us who had known and admired the German naval officers in the happy pre-war days, their organisation, equipment, and fighting spirit were deeply admired by everybody in the Fleet. We fought with no mean enemy and the humiliation of the surrender at Scapa was no fitting end for such men and such ships.

One other sea picture before I close this record of our life afloat. On board a P. & O. ship in the bitter winter weather of January 1917, I am sharing the top of the radiator in the smoking room with a passenger belonging to the Malay States Civil Service. In accordance with the routine of his department, war or no war, he has been spending his six months' leave in England and is now returning. It is night-time, nearly 11 o'clock, and the ship is zig-zagging her way down the murky channel on our first night at sea. There is something on my companion's mind and has been ever since we had seen the glare and heard the thunder of the explosion of the munition factory outside Southend the night before. We had been lying at anchor off the Nore, as all traffic in the Thames was forbidden after dark.

'Are you going to bed to-night?' he asks.

'Yes, of course.'

'Are you going to take off all your clothes?'

'Yes.'

'Aren't you frightened?'

'The bulging tyre of the Gieve waistcoat which he is wearing has been gradually rendering my position on top of the narrow radiator untenable, and I get up.

'Look here! I've been so frightened for the past two and a half years that I cannot be frightened any more. Good-night.'

THE END